# The Comprehensive
# Study of Music
## ANTHOLOGY OF MUSIC FROM PLAINCHANT THROUGH GABRIELI

# THE COMPREHENSIVE STUDY OF MUSIC
## ANTHOLOGY OF MUSIC FROM PLAINCHANT THROUGH GABRIELI

*William Brandt*
Washington State University

*Arthur Corra*
Illinois State University

*William Christ*

*Richard DeLone*

*Allen Winold*
Indiana University

## VOLUME I

**HARPER & ROW, PUBLISHERS**
NEW YORK   HAGERSTOWN   PHILADELPHIA   SAN FRANCISCO   LONDON

Sponsoring Editor: Phillip Leininger
Project Editor: Bob Ginsberg
Production Manager: Kewal K. Sharma
Compositor: Armando Dal Molin, Music Typographers
Printer and Binder: The Murray Printing Company

**THE COMPREHENSIVE STUDY OF MUSIC, Volume I**
ANTHOLOGY OF MUSIC FROM PLAINCHANT THROUGH GABRIELI

Copyright © 1980 by Harper & Row, Publishers, Inc.

Library of Congress Cataloging in Publication Data

Main entry under title:

Anthology of music from plainchant through Gabrieli.

    (The Comprehensive study of music; v. 1)
    Includes indexes.
    1. Chants (Plain, Gregorian, etc.)  2. Vocal
music.  3. Instrumental music.  I. Brandt,
William E.  II. Series.
M2.C67  vol. 1 [M5] [M1495]  780'.8s [780'.82]
ISBN 0-06-040922-3         79-9159

# ACKNOWLEDGEMENTS

"Io non compro piu speranza" by Marco Cara from *Le Frottole per Canto e Liuto Intabulate da Franciscus Bossinensis*, ed. by Benvenuto Disertori, Vol. 3, pp. 390–391. Copyright © 1964 by G. Ricordi & C.S.p.A. Milan, by kind permission of G. Ricordi & C.S.p.A. Publishers owners.

"Che pena è quest' al cor" by Francesco Landini from *Keyboard Music of the Late Middle Ages in Codex Faenza 117*, ed. by Dragan Plamenac; "Ave Maris Stella" by Guillaume Dufay from *Guillaume Dufay, Opera Omnia*, vol. 5, ed. by Heinrich Besseler; "Se la face ay pale" by Guillaume Dufay from *Guillaume Dufay, Opera Omnia*, vol. 6, ed. by Heinrich Besseler; *Missa Se la face ay pale* (Kyrie) by Guillaume Dufay from *Guillaume Dufay, Opera Omnia*, vol. 3, ed. by Heinrich Besseler; "Ce jour de l'an" by Guillaume Dufay from *Guillaume Dufay, Opera Omnia*, vol. 6, ed. by Heinrich Besseler; "Il bianco e dolce cigno" by Jacob Arcadelt from *Jacobus Arcadelt, Opera Omnia*, vol. 2, ed. by Albert Seay; "O Magnum Mysterium' by Adrian Willaert from *Adrian Willaert, Sämtliche Werke*, vol. 1, ed. by Hermann Zensk; "O Magnum Mysterium" by Giovanni Gabrieli from *Giovanni Gabrieli, Opera Omnia*, vol. 1, ed. by Denis Arnold; "Revecy venir du printemps" by Claude Le Jeune from *Claude LeJeune Airs*, vol. 1, ed. by D. P. Walker. Permissions by Dr. Armen Carapetyan, Director of the American Institute of Musicology, Florence, Italy.

"Viderunt omnes" by Perotin from *The Works of Perotin* by Ethel Thurston. Copyright 1970 by Belwin-Mills Publishing Corp. Used by permission.

"Ein' feste Burg" (1&2) by Johann Walther from *Johann Walter, Sämtliche Werke*, vol. 1, ed. by Otto Schröder; "Ein' feste Burg ist unser Gott" by Johann Walther from *Johann Walther, Sämtliche Werke*, vol. 3, ed. by Otto Schröder. Copyright by Concrodia Publishing House. Reprinted by permission.

*Tertia Missa in Nativitate Domini Nostri Jesu Christi*, Anonymous. Permission by Desclée Editeurs, Tournai, Belgium.

"Qui es promesses/Ha! Fortune/Et non est qui adjuvet" by Guillaume de Machaut from *Polyphonic Music of the Fourteenth Century*, vol. 2, ed. by Leo Schrade; "Honte, paour, doubtance" by Guillaume de Machaut from *Polyphonic Music of the Fourteenth Century*, vol. 3, ed. by Leo Schrade; "Douce dame jolie" and "Rose, liz, printemps verdure" by Guillaume de Machuat from *Polypohonic Music from the Fourteenth Century*, vol. 3, ed. by Leo Schrade; "Fenice fu'" by Jacopo da Bologna from *Polyphonic Music of the Fourteenth Century*, vol. 6, ed. by W. Thomas Marrocco; "Con brachi assai" by Giovanni da Firenze from *Polyphonic Music of the Fourteenth Century*, vol.6, ed. by W. Thomas Marrocco. Permissions by Editions de l'oiseau-lyre, Monaco.

"Viderunt Hemanuel," Anonymous. Reprinted by permission of the publishers from *Historical Anthology of Music*, Volume 1, by Archibald T. Davison and Willi Apel, Cambridge, Mass.: Harvard University Press, Copyright © 1946, 1949 by the President and Fellows of Harvard College; © renewed 1974 by Alice D. Humez and Willi Apel.

"Amor vittorioso" by Giovanni Gastoldi from *G. G. Gastoldi, Balletti a cinque voci*, ed. by Michel Sanvoisin. Published with the authorization of Heugel & Cie., Music Publishers, Paris.

"Prendés i garde" by Guillaume d'Amiens from *Troubadors, Trouvéres, Minne- and Meistersinger*, ed. by Friedrich Gennrich. Permission by MCA Music, New York.

"Petite Nymphe folastre" by Clement Janequin from *European Madrigals*, ed. by Egon Kraus. Permission by Musikverlag zum Pelikan, Zurich.

"Flow My Tears" by John Dowland from *The English Lute-Songs*, Series I, 5 & 6, ed. by Edmund Fellowes, revised by Thurston Dart; "Ye Sacred Muses" by William Byrd from *The Collected Works of William Byrd*, vol. 15, Consort Songs, ed. by Philip Brett. Used with permission of Stainer & Bell, Ltd., copyright holder.

"Sing we to this merry company," Anonymous, from "Medieval Carols," *Musica Britannica*, vol. 4, 2nd revised ed., ed. by John Stevens; "Ave maris stella" by John Dunstable from "John Dunstable's Complete Works," *Musica Britannica*, vol. 8, ed. by Manfred Bukofzer. Used with permission of Stainer & Bell, Ltd., © Musica Britannica trust.

"Absolon, fili mi" by Josquin des Près from *Werken van Josquin des Près*, No. 55, Supplement, ed. by M. Antonowycz & W. Elders, Amsterdam 1969; "Faulte d'argent" by Josquin des Près from *Werken van Josquin des Près*, No. 5, Wereldlijke werken II, ed. by A. Smijers, Amsterdam 924; "Deploration sur la mort d'Ockeghem" by Josquin des Près from *Werken van Josquin des Près*, No. 5, Wereldlijke werken II, ed. by A. Smijers, Amsterdam 1924; *Missa Ave maris stella* (Kyrie and Agnus Dei) by Josquin des Près from *Werken van Josquin des Près*, Amsterdam 1935. Permission by Vereniging voor Nederlandse Muziekgeschiedenis, Amsterdam.

"Viderunt omnes" by Leonin from *The Rhythm of Twelfth-Century Polyphony* by William Waite, vol. 2, Yale Studies in the History of Music, 1954. Permission by Yale University Press.

"Fantasia No. 8" by Luis de Milan from *El Maestro*, tran. & ed. by Charles Jacobs, Penn State, copyright © 1971 The Pennsylvania State University. All rights reserved.

*In ecclesiis* by Gabrieli, ed. by Denis Stevens, Penn State Music Series, Courtesy The Pennsylvania State University. All right reserved.

"Toccata" by Jan Sweelinck from *Werken van Jan Peiterszn Sweelinck*, vol. 1, ed. by Max Seiffert & Martinus Nijhoff. Reprint permission granted by the publisher and copyright owner G. Alsbach & Co.

"Quem queritis in presepe," and "Gaudeamus hodie quia Deus," in Paul Evans *The Early Trope Repertory of St. Martial de Limoges* (© 1970 by Princeton University Press), pp. 129 and 130. Reprinted by permission of Princeton University Press.

*The Play of Herod, A Twelfth-Century Musical Drama*, Anonymous, ed. by Noah Greenberg and William L. Smoldon. Copyright © 1964, 1965 by Noah Greenberg and William L. Smoldon. Reprinted by permission of Oxford University Press, Inc.

"Prologo & Cantiga 1" by Alfonso el Sabio from *La Música de las Cantigas de Santa María del rey Alfonso el Sabio*, vol. 2, ed. by H. Anglés. Diputacíon Provencial de Barcelona. Reprinted by permission.

"Diferencias sobre Canto del Cavallero" by Antonio de Cabezón from *Obras de musica para tecla, arpa y vihuela*, vol. 3, ed. by Felip Pedrell, new ed. by Higinio Anglés; "O Magnum Mysterium" by Tomás Luis de Victoria from *Tomás Luis de Victoria*, *Opera Omnia*, vol. 25–26, Motetes I–XXI, ed. by Higinio Anglés. Consejo Superior de Investigaciones Científicas. Reprinted by permission.

# CONTENTS

*viii*  Contents

# ALPHABETICAL LIST OF COMPOSERS

# FOREWORD TO THE SERIES

The history, literature, theory, and performance of music are all aspects of one indivisible whole. Unfortunately, in most introductory courses as they are taught today, there is little apparent sense of how intimately related they are. In general, a schism has developed in the training of musicians that has resulted in the compartmentalization of the materials of music into subjects taught (often out of sequence and independently) by different departments. Few attempts are made to wed these elements as they are indissolubly wed in the on-going stream of music history and performance.

However, since the pioneering efforts of the Juilliard School (in its "Literature and Materials" course) and of subsequent work done by the School of Music, Indiana University, and by other institutions taking part in the Ford Foundation Contemporary Music Project (CMP), forward-looking music educators have realized the importance of reuniting the theoretical materials of music with music history and literature, and with aspects of performance. The experimentation with the new methodology demonstrated conclusively (but not really surprisingly) that integrated study of the materials of music is virtually impossible without a set of instructional materials that are well-organized and that cover each area adequately. Ideally, courses designed for such comprehensive study should not only develop the knowledge of how music is constructed, but should also trace the evolution of musical styles, performance practices, and music history and literature in a logical, coherent sequence.

Challenged by the difficulty and importance of creating suitable materials for such a coordinated approach, we have developed *The Comprehensive Study of Music*—a series of anthologies of musical works, theory and history textbooks, and other instructional materials that provide an integrated program of study for undergraduate music majors.

The basic goals of *The Comprehensive Study of Music* are to assist the student of music in acquiring knowledge of:

1. Important musical works representing the historical and theoretical aspects of music
2. The sociocultural contexts from which the works emerged
3. The intrinsic characteristics of individual works and the basic principles they share with works of other styles, periods, and genres
4. The techniques of analysis, writing, and listening that evolve from the study of music literature
5. Significant composers and their works within the context of the major developments in music
6. The techniques and skills needed for music reading, dictation, and keyboard harmony

The scope of the program is large, embracing most of the activities or disciplines traditionally associated with music study—analysis, writing, reading, performing, improvising, listening, and doing research on theoretical and historical subjects. Though we cover many genres, styles, and works, we believe it will be more helpful for the student to penetrate deeply into a limited number of works than to study many superficially. Another of the most important themes throughout *The Comprehensive Study of Music* is the relation between academic and applied music studies, and we make frequent suggestions regarding ways theoretical and historical matters may be related to performance practice.

Last, though the series is designed for use in courses in which at least some aspects of instruction in music theory and music literature are integrated, individual volumes may also be used in separate courses in each of these disciplines. The complete series contains the following:

Anthologies of Music

Volume I       *From Plainchant Through Gabrieli* (available now)
Volume II      *From Monteverdi Through Mozart* (available now)
Volume III     *From Beethoven Through Wagner* (available now)
Volume IV      *From Debussy Through Stockhausen* (available now)
Volume V       *Piano Reductions for Harmonic Study* (available now)

Core Texts for History and Theory

Volume VI      *Basic Principles of Music Theory* (available now)
Volume VII     *Plainchant Through Gabrieli* (forthcoming))
Volume VIII    *Monteverdi Through Mozart* (forthcoming)
Volume IX      *Beethoven Through Wagner* (forthcoming)
Volume X       *Debussy Through Stockhausen* (forthcoming)

Additional Materials

Volume XI      *Melodic Ear Training and Sight Reading* (forthcoming)
Volume XII     *Harmony Ear Training and Keyboard Realization* (forthcoming)

The Authors

# PREFACE

This anthology is the first of a series of four, the music of which forms the nucleus of *The Comprehensive Study of Music,* a coordinated approach to the materials, structure, literature, and history of music. Other music anthologies of the series are as follows:

*Anthology of Music from Monteverdi through Mozart*
*Anthology of Music from Beethoven through Wagner*
*Anthology of Music from Debussy through Stockhausen*

(In addition, there is a fifth book, *Piano Reductions for Harmonic Study,* which is derived from the works appearing in the four music anthologies.)

The four music anthologies focus on the music of Western civilization, encompassing a wide variety of musical forms, types, and styles, and representative works of prominent composers. Being chronologically arranged, this significant collection affords a panoramic view of compositional and stylistic practices in important types of art music from early chant through music of today. The examples, mostly of complete works, illustrate the various important genres of music—instrumental and vocal, solo and ensemble (both small and large), and sacred and secular. Included are toccatas, ballades, motets, masses, fugues, concertos, chorales, songs, symphonies, sonatas, opera excerpts, piano pieces, chamber works, and other types as well.

These four anthologies provide the essential music literature for the study of music theory, including such basics as cantus firmus technique, chords, progressions, modulation, texture, contrapuntal devices, developmental techniques, tonality (its development and subsequent dissolution), serialism, and aleatory.

The anthologies contain works exemplifying prevalent musical forms and stylistic practices of the major periods of music history, thus affording a concise survey of the vast body of standard works in many styles, in various genres, and for different performance media. In relatively limited space, then, a full, versatile sampling of some of the most important forms of music is provided, musical works often representing milestones in the historical development of the art form.

In contrast to many such collections, the music contained in these anthologies was chosen with an eye toward ease of performance for both student and teacher. And those few works that may unduly challenge performance skills are readily available on commercial recording. In addition to its pedagogical value, we believe this collection of music—so valuable for the basic study of history, literature, and theory—because of its intrinsic worth, should become a permanent part of the reference library of every serious student of music.

The fifth book, *Piano Reductions for Harmonic Study,* was developed as a pedagogical aid in the use of the music anthologies. It consists of simple, playable, easy-to-find reductions of excerpts from the music contained in the anthologies, excerpts chosen to illustrate common theoretical materials, techniques and practices. These reductions of selected examples provide a ready source of materials for study and illustration, thus minimizing the difficulties of finding specific examples and of performing from a full score.

While the anthologies were conceived as the foundation of an integrated study of music history, literature, and theory, resourceful students and teachers will find other uses for them. For example, the music anthologies can be used as the basis for the study of form and analysis or as supplementary materials for classes in keyboard and sight singing. The *Anthology of Music from Debussy through Stockhausen* can provide the foundation for study of the techniques of twentieth-century music. The anthologies can be used in conjunction with various harmony texts. In such cases, the *Piano Reductions for Harmonic Study* would be a most valuable addition. In other words, because of the breadth and scope of the materials developed for *The Comprehensive Study of Music*, the possibilities of usage are many and varied.

Lastly, we believe that thorough knowledge of, and familiarity with, the intrinsic characteristics of the works contained in the aforementioned anthologies will afford students a comprehensive view of the practices of Western art music.

# TERTIA MISSA IN NATIVITATE DOMINI NOSTRI JESU CHRISTI

ANONYMOUS

# THIRD MASS FOR CHRISTMAS DAY

INTROIT: PUER NATUS EST (MODE 7)

*ANONYMOUS*

Pu - er na - tus est no - bis, et fi - li - us da - tus est no -

bis: cu - jus im - pe - ri - um su - per hu - me rum e - jus et

vo - ca - bi - tur no - men e - jus, mag - ni con - si - li - i An - ge - lus.

[Psalm]

Can - ta - te Do - mi - no can - ti - cum no - vum: qui - a mi - ra - bi - li - a fe - cit.

Glo - ri - a Pa - tri et fi - li - o, et Spi - ri - tu - i San - cto. Si - cut e - rat in prin - ci - pi - o,

et nunc et sem - per, et in sae - cu - la sae - cu - lo - rum, A - men.

A child is born to us, and a Son is given to us: whose government is upon His shoulder: and His name shall be called, the Angel of great counsel. [Ps.] Sing ye to the Lord a new canticle: because He has done wonderful things. [℣.] Glory be to the Father, and to the Son, and to the Holy Spirit, as it was in the beginning, is now, and ever shall be, world without end. Amen.

Ky - ri - e        *        e  -  le  - i - son, Ky - ri - e        e  -

-  le  - i - son, Ky - ri - e        e  -  le  -  i - son Chri - ste

e  -  le - i - son, Chri - ste        e  -  le  -  i - son, Chri - ste

e  -  le - i - son.  Ky - ri - e

e  -  le - i - son, Ky - ri - e        e  -        le - i - son, Ky - ri - e

e  -  le  -  i - son.

Lord, have mercy; Lord, have mercy; Lord, have mercy.
Christ, have mercy; Christ, have mercy; Christ, have mercy.
Lord, have mercy; Lord, have mercy; Lord, have mercy.

4 *Anonymous*

Tu so-lus Al - tis - si - mus, Je - su Chri - ste. Cum Sanc-to Spi - ri - tu,

in glo - ri - a De - i Pa - tris. A - men.

Glory be to God on high, and on earth, peace to men of good will. We praise you, we bless you, we adore you, we glorify you. We give thanks for your great glory. O Lord, heavenly King, God the Almighty Father. The only begotten Son of God, Jesus Christ. Lord God, Lamb of God, Son of the Father. You who take away the sins of the world, have mercy upon us. You who take away the sins of the world, receive our prayers. You who sits at the right hand of the Father, have mercy upon us. For you alone are Holy. You alone are the Lord. You alone are the Most High, Jesus Christ, with the Holy Spirit in the glory of God the Father. Amen.

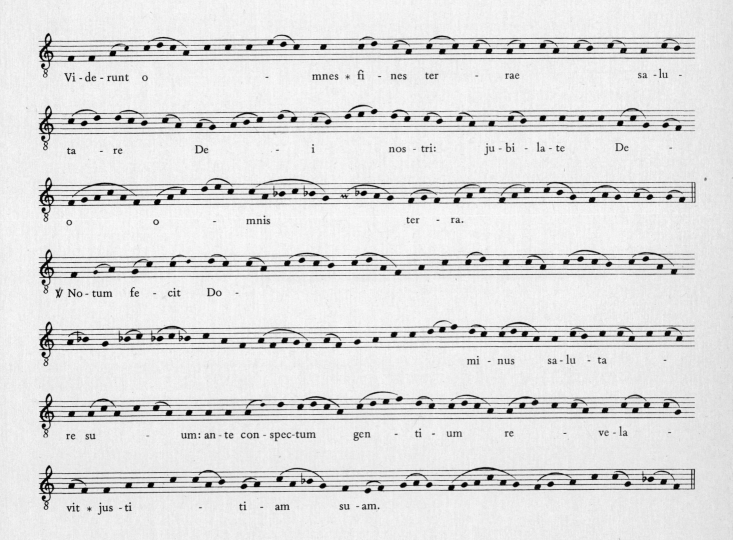

All the ends of the earth have seen the salvation of our God: sing joyfully to God, all the earth. [V.] The Lord has made known His salvation: in the sight of the nations He has revealed His justice.

Alleluia, alleluia. [℣.] A sanctified day has dawned upon us: come you nations and adore the Lord: for this day a great light has descended upon the earth. Alleluia.

8 *Anonymous*

*Contrast to the others — long and syllabic.*

Cre - do in u - num De - um, Pa - trem om - ni - pot - en - tem, fa - cto - rem cae - li et ter - rae,

vi - si - bi - li - um om - ni - um, et in - vi - si - bi - li - um. Et in u - num Do - mi -

num Je - sum Chris - tum, Fi - li - um De - i u - ni - ge - ni - tum. Et ex Pa - tre na - tum

an - te om - ni - a sae - cu - la. De - um de De - o, lu - men de lu - mi - ne,

De - um ve - rum de De - o ve - ro. Ge - ni - tum, non fac - tum, con - sub - stan - ti - a - lem

Pa - tri: per quem om - ni - a fac - ta sunt. Qui pro - pter nos ho - mi - nes

et pro - pter no - stram sa - lu - tem de - scen - dit de cae - lis. Et in - car - na - tus est

de Spi - ri - tu San - cto ex Ma - ri - a Vir - gi - ne: Et ho - mo fa - ctus est.

Cru - ci - fi - xus et - i - am pro no - bis: sub Pon - ti - o Pi - la - to pas - sus, et

se - pul - tus est. Et re - sur - re - xit ter - ti - a di - e, se - cun - dum Scrip - tu - ras.

Et as - cen - dit in cae - lum: se - det ad dex - te - ram Pa - tris. Et i - te - rum ven - tu -

rus est cum glo-ri-a, ju-di-ca-re vi-vos et mor-tu-os: cu-jus

re-gni non e-rit fi-nis. Et in Spi-ri-tum Sanc-tam, Do-mi-num, et vi-

vi-fi-can-tem: qui ex Pa-tre Fi-li-o-que pro-ce-dit. Qui cum Pa-tre et

Fi-li-o si-mul a-do-ra-tur, et con-glo-ri-fi-ca-tur: qui lo-cu-tus

est per Pro-phe-tas. Et u-nam sanc-tam ca-tho-li-cam et a-pos-

to-li-cam Ec-cle-si-am. Con-fi-te-or u-num bap-tis-ma in re-mis-

si-o-nem pec-ca-to-rum. Et ex-spec-to re-sur-rec-ti-o-nem mor-tu-o-

rum. Et vi-tam ven-tu-ri sae-cu-li. A - men.

I believe in one God, the Father Almighty, maker of heaven and earth, and of all things visible and invisible. And in one Lord Jesus Christ, the only-begotten Son of God. Born of the Father before all ages. God of God; light of light; true God of true God. Begotten not made; of one being with the Father; by whom all things were made. Who for us men, and for our salvation, came down from heaven. And was made flesh by the Holy Spirit of the Virgin Mary; and was made man. He also was crucified for us: suffered under Pontius Pilate and was buried. And on the third day He rose again according to the Scriptures. And ascending into heaven, He sits at the right hand of the Father. And He shall come again in glory to judge the living and the dead: and of His kingdom there shall be no end. And I believe in the Holy Spirit, Lord and giver of life, who proceeds from the Father and the Son. Who together with the Father and the Son is no less adored, and glorified: who spoke by the Prophets. And I believe in One, holy, catholic and apostolic church. I confess one baptism for the remission of sins. And I look for the resurrection of the dead. And the life of the world to come. Amen.

10 Anonymous

Yours are the heavens, and yours is the earth, the world and the fullness thereof you have founded: justice and judgment are the preparation of your throne.

## Sanctus (mode 4)

San - - - ctus, * San - ctus, San - - ctus Do - mi - nus De - us

sa - ba - oth. Ple - ni sunt cae - li et ter - ra glo - - ri - a tu - a.

Ho - san - - na in ex - cel - sis. Be - ne - dic - tus qui ve - nit in no -

mi - ne Do - mi - ni. Ho - - san - - na in ex - cel - sis.

Holy, holy, holy, Lord God of Hosts. Heaven and earth are filled with your glory. Hosanna in the highest heaven. Blessed is He who comes in the name of the Lord. Hosanna in the highest heaven.

12 *Anonymous*

A - gnus De - i, * qui tol - lis pec - ca - ta

mun - di: mi - se - re - re no - bis. A - gnus De - i * qui tol - lis

pec - ca - ta mun - di: mi - se - re - re no - bis. A - gnus De - i, *

qui tol - lis pec - ca - ta mun - di: do - na no - bis pa - cem.

Lamb of God, who takes away the sins of the world, have mercy on us.
Lamb of God, who takes away the sins of the world, have mercy on us.
Lamb of God, who takes away the sins of the world, grant us peace.

Vi - de - runt om - nes. * Fi - nes ter - rae sa - lu -
ta - re De - i no - stri.

All the ends of the earth have seen the salvation of our God.

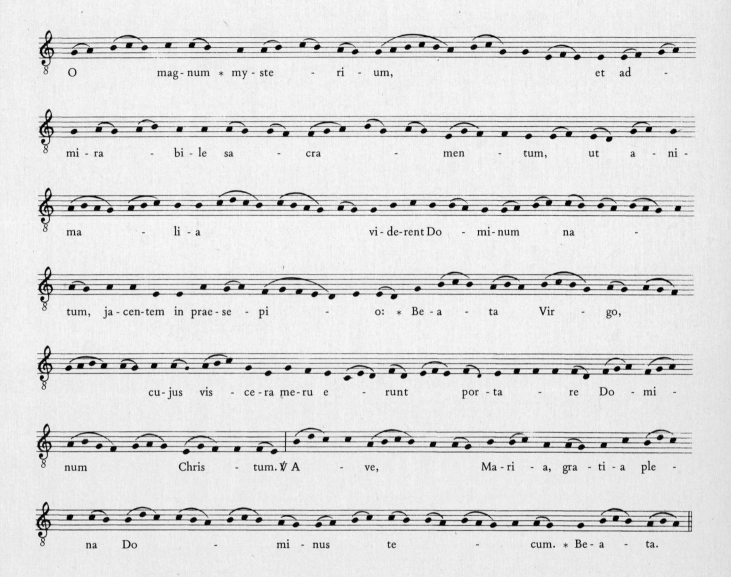

O great mystery and admirable sacrament, that the animals should witness the birth of the Lord, lowly, in a stable.

Blessed Virgin, whose womb was worthy to bear the Lord, Christ!

Hail, Mary, full of grace: the Lord is with you.

Blessed Virgin ...

An - ge - lus * ad pas - to - res a — it: An - nun - ti - o vo - bis gau - di - um

mag-num: qui - a na - tus est vo - bis ho — di — e sal - va - tor mun - di, al - le - lu - ia.

1. De — us De — us me — us * ad te de lu — ce vi - gi - lo

*Flex:* inaquosa: †

The angel said to the shepherds: I speak to you with great joy: because today the savior of the world is born to you. Alleluia.

1 O God, you are my God, early will I seek you.

2 Sitivit in te ánima méa,* quam multi-pliciter tibi cáro méa!

2 My soul thirsts for you, my flesh longs for you.

3 In térra desérta et invia et inaquósa: † sic in sáncto appárui tibi,* ut vidérem virtútem túam, et glóriam túam.

3 As a parched and lifeless land without water: thus have I gazed toward you in the sanctuary, to see your power and your glory, so as I have seen you in the sanctuary.

4 Quóniam mélior est misericórdia túa super vitas:* lábia méa laudábunt te.

4 Because your lovingkindness is better than life, my lips shall praise you.

5 Sic benedicam te in vita méa:* et in nómine túo levábo mánus méas.

5 Thus will I bless you while I live: in your name I will lift up in my hands.

6 Sicut ádipe et pinguédine repleátur ánima méa:* et lábiis exsultatiónis laudábit os méum.

6 As with fatness and marrow my soul shall be satisfied; and with exultant lips my mouth shall praise you.

7 Si mémor fúi túi super strátum méum, † in matutinis meditábor in te:* quia fuisti adjútor méus.

7 I will remember you upon my bed, and through the night-watches meditate on you: because you have been my help.

8 Et in velaménto alárum tuárum exsultábo, † adhaésit ánima méa post te:* me suscépit déxtera túa.

8 And in the shadow of your wings will I rejoice, my soul clings fast to you; your right hand upholds me.

9 Ipsi vero in vánum quaesiérunt ánimam méam, † introibunt in inferióra térrae:* tradéntur in mánus gládii, pártes vúlpium érunt.

9 But those that seek to destroy my soul, shall go into the depths of the earth: they shall fall by the sword, they shall be the prey of foxes.

*16 Anonymous*

Ho - di - e * Chris - tus na - tus est: ho - di - e Sal - va - tor ap - pa - ru - it: ho - di - e in ter - ra ca - nunt An - ge - li, lae - tan - tur Arch - an - ge - li: ho - di - e ex - sul - tant jus - ti, di - cen - tes: Glo - ri - a in ex - cel - sis De - o, al - le - lu - ia. E u o u a e.

This day Christ was born: this day the Savior appeared: this day the Angels sing on earth, and the Archangels rejoice: this day the just exult, saying: Glory to God in the highest, alleluia.

10 Rex vero laetábitur in Déo, †
laudabúntur ómnes qui júrant in éo:*
quia obstrúctum est os loquéntium
iniqua.

10 However the king shall rejoice in God,
everyone who swears by him shall
glory: but the mouth of those who
speak lies shall be stopped.

11 Glória Pátri, et Filio,* et Spiritui
Sáncto.

11 Glory to the Father, and to the Son,
and to the Holy Spirit.

12 Sicut érat in principio, et núnc, et
sémper,* et in saécula saeculórum.
Amen.

12 As it was in the beginning, is now, and
ever shall be, world without end.
Amen.

# TROPES TO THE INTROIT: PUER NATUS EST

QUEM QUERITIS IN PRESEPE

*ANONYMOUS*

Quem que - ri - tis in pre - se - pe, pas - to - res, di - ci - te?

Sal - va - to - rem Xpis-tum Do - mi - num, in - fan - tem pan -

nis in - vo - lu - tum se - cun - dum ser - mo - nem an - ge - li - cum.

Ad - est hic par - vu - lus cum Ma - ri - a ma - tre su - a,

de qua du - dum va - ti - ci - nan - do I - sa - i - as di - xe - rat

pro - phe - ta: "Ec - ce vir - go con - ci - pi - et et pa - ri - et

fi - li - um." Et nunc e - un - tes di - ci - te qui - a na - tus est.

AL - LE - LU - IA, al - le - lu - ia. Iam ve - re sci - mus Xpis-tum na - tum

Puer natus est

in ter - ris, de quo ca - ni - te om - nes cum pro - phe - ta di - cen-tes:

Whom do you seek in the manger, shepherds, tell us?
The Savior, Christ, the Lord, an infant wrapped in tattered cloth, according to the words
    of the angel.
Here is a small child with Mary, his mother, about whom, long ago, the prophet Isaiah,
    prophesying, said: "Behold, virgin, you shall conceive and bear a son."
And now go forth and tell why he is born.
Alleluia. Alleluia.
At last we truly know that Christ has been born on earth, of whom everyone sings with
    the prophet, saying: (A child is born . . .)

GAUDEAMUS HODIE QUIA DEUS

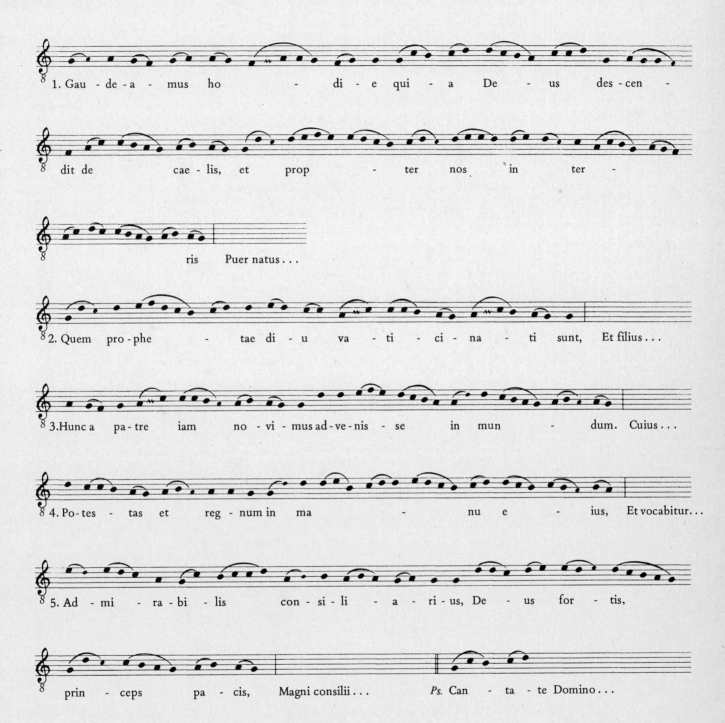

1. Gau - de - a - mus ho - di - e qui - a De - us des - cen -

dit de cae - lis, et prop - ter nos in - ter -

ris Puer natus . . .

2. Quem pro - phe - tae di - u va - ti - ci - na - ti sunt, Et filius . . .

3. Hunc a pa - tre iam no - vi - mus ad - ve - ni - se in mun - dum. Cuius . . .

4. Po - tes - tas et reg - num in ma - nu e - ius, Et vocabitur . . .

5. Ad - mi - ra - bi - lis con - si - li - a - ri - us, De - us for - tis,

prin - ceps pa - cis, Magni consilii . . . *Ps.* Can - ta - te Domino . . .

1 We rejoice today because God has descended from heaven, and come to us on earth.
(A child is born . . .)
2 Whom the prophets had foretold long ago, (and a Son . . .)
3 Hence from the Father we know now He came into the world. (Whose government . . .)
4 Power and authority in his hand: (and His name . . .)
5 Wonderful counsellor, powerful God, prince of peace, (the Angel of great counsel . . .)
(Sing ye . . .)

*TROPES TO THE INTROIT: PUER NATUS EST 19*

# PROSA FOR CHRISTMAS

NATO CANUNT OMNIA DOMINO (MODE 8)

Na - to ca - nunt o - mni - a Do - mi - no pi - a ag - mi - na. Syl - la - ba - tim neu - ma - ta

per - strin - gen - do or - ga - ni - ca. Hac di - e sa - cra - ta in qua no - va sunt gau - di - a

mun - do ple - na de - di - ta. Hac noc - te prae - cel - sa in - to - nu - it et glo - ri - a

in vo - ce an - ge - li - ca Ful - se - runt et im - ma - ni - a noc - te me - di - a

pa - sto - ri - bus lu - mi - na, Dum fo - vent su - a pec - to - ra sub - i - to di - va

per - ci - pi - unt mo - ni - ta. Na - tus al - ma vir - gi - ne, qui ex - stat an - te sae - cu - la.

Est im - men - sa in cae - lo glo - ri - a pax et in ter - ra sic er - go cae - li

ca - ter - va al - tis - si - me iu - bi - la, ut tan - to ca - no - re tre - mat al - ta po - li

ma - chi - na. So - net et per o - mni - a hac in di - e glo - ri - a vo - ce cla - ra

re - di - ta. Hu - ma - na con - cre - pent cun - cta De - um na - tum in ter - ra. Con - fra - cta sunt

im - pe - ri - a ho - stis cru - de - lis - si - ma. Pax in cae - lo glo - ri - a, nunc lae - ten - tur

o - mni - a    na - ti per ex - or - di - na.    So - lus qui tu - e - tur o - mni - a,    So - lus qui con -

di - dit o - mni - a,    I - pse su - a pi - e - ta - te    sal - vet o - mni - a pec - ca - to reg - na.

"He is born," everyone sings, the God-fearing throng.

Syllabically and neumatically, bound together musically.

This holy day, in which joys are renewed, the world is full of devotion.

This magnificent night, they make a thundering noise, giving glory in angelic voices.

Shining and vast, in the middle of the night, a light was seen by shepherds.

While tending their sheep, they suddenly understood the divine prophecies.

Born (to this) gracious virgin, who appears before all ages.

Glory is boundless in heaven and on earth peace.

So therefore in heaven, the crowd in highest joy,

With much singing causes the high heaven to tremble.

It sounds and through all, this day in glory, in a clear voice resounds.

All humanity makes a noise, God is born on earth.

Broken are the commands of the cruelest enemy.

Peace and glory in heaven, now all rejoice, born in good order.

Who alone beholds all, who alone established all,

His own piousness saves everyone from the power of sin.

# THE PLAY OF HEROD

SCENE I: ANGELS AND SHEPHERDS

Scene 1: Angels and Shepherds

*At the sound of the bell preceding "Nolite timere vos," the Shepherds turn with fear, looking up to the Archangel.*

Here begins the Book of the Representation, "Herod." Herod and the other members of the cast being ready to go on, then let the Angel appear above with a multitude of other Angels. Seeing this, the Shepherds are afraid. While the other Angels still remain silent, let the Angels sing greetings:

in - vo - lú - tum et_ pó - si - tum_ in_ prae - sé - pi - o

in _ me - di - o du - um_ a - ni - ma - li _ um. _

No longer be afraid! For behold, I bring you good tidings of great joy which shall be to all people; for unto us is born this day in the city of David a Savior of the world, and this shall be a sign: You shall find the babe wrapped in swaddling clothes lying in a manger between two beasts.

*The Shepherds, facing the Angels, fall to their knees.*
And suddenly let all the multitude with the Angel say;

Bells

Angel Choir

Glo - ri - a in ex - cél - sis De - o! _

et in ter - ra _ pax ho - mi - ni - bus bo - nae

vo - lun - tá - tis; al - le - lú - ia, al - le - lú - ia!

Glory be to God on high, and on earth, peace to men of good will; alleluia, alleluia.

Then let the Shepherds, arising, sing to each other:

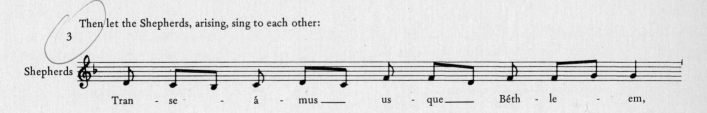

Shepherds

Tran - se - á - mus _ us - que _ Béth - le _ em,

et __ vi - de - á __ mus __ hoc __ ver - bum quod fac __ tum __ est,

quod __ fe - cit Dó - mi - nus et __ os - tén - dit no - bis.

Let us go to Bethlehem, and see this thing which has come to pass, which the Lord has done and made known to us.

And thus let them proceed as far as the Manger which has been prepared at the monastery doors, and then let two women guarding the Manger question the Shepherds, saying:

**4**

Bells

Midwives

Quem __ quáe - ri - tis, pás - to - res, dí - ci - te? _____

Whom do you seek, shepherds, tell us?

**5** Let the Shepherds reply:

Shepherds

Sal - va - tó - rem __ Chri - stum Dó - - mi - num;

In - fán - tem __ pan - nis in - vo - lú - tum,

se - cún - dum sér - mo - nem __ an - gé - li - cum.

The Savior, Jesus Christ, the Lord; The infant wrapped in swaddling clothes, according to the words of the angel.

24 | *Anonymous*

6 The women:

Bells

1st Midwife

A - dest hic ———— pár - - vu - lus

cum Ma - ri - a ———— ma - tre ———— e - ius,

2nd Midwife

de qua ——— du - dum ——— va - ti - ci - nan - do

Y - sa - í - as pro - phé - ta ——— di - xe - rat:

Both Midwives

"Ec - ce ——— vir - go ——— con - cí - pi - et

et pá - ri et fí - li - um!"

Behold! Here with Mary his mother is the little child, whose coming the prophet Isaiah long ago foretold, saying: "Behold, a virgin shall conceive and shall bear a son!"

# CAN VEI LA LAUZETA MOVER

TROUBADOUR CANZO                                      *BERNART DE VENTADORN*

Reading pg 69

Can vei la lauzeta mover
De joi sas alas contra ·l rai,
Que s'oblid'e ·s laissa chazer
Per la doussor c'al cor li vai,
Ailas! quals enveja m'en ve
De cui qu'eu veja jauzion!
Meravilhas ai, quar desse
Lo cors de dezirer no ·m fon.

Ailas! tan cuidava saber
D'amor, e tan petit en sai,
Car¸eu d'amar no ·m posc tener
Celeis don ja pro non aurai.
Tout m'a mon cor, e tout m'a se

When I see the lark
Spread its wings for joy and fly towards the sun,
Forget itself, and fall
In the bliss that rushes to its heart
Alas! how I then envy
All creatures that I see happy.
I am amazed that my heart
Does not melt away there and then with longing.

Alas! how much of love I thought I knew
And how little I know;
For I cannot stop loving
Her from whom I may have nothing.
All my heart, and all herself,

| | |
|---|---|
| E se mezeis e tot lo mon; | And all my own self and all I have |
| E can se •m tolc, no •m laisset re | She has taken from me, and leaves me nothing |
| Mas dezirer e cor volon. | But longing and a seeking heart. |

| | |
|---|---|
| Anc non agui de me poder | I no longer had power over myself, |
| Ni no fui meus, de l'or en sai | Nor belonged to myself, from the moment |
| Que •m laisset en sos olhs vezer, | When she let me look into her eyes; |
| En un miralh que mout me plai. | Into that mirror which so delights me. |
| Miralhs, pus me mirei en te, | Mirror, since I was mirrored in you |
| M'an mort li sospir de preon, | My sighs have slain me; |
| C'aissi •m perdei com perdet se | I am lost |
| Lo bels Narcisus en la fon. | As fair Narcissus was lost in the spring. |

| | |
|---|---|
| De las domnas me dezesper; | I despair of all women; |
| Ja mais en lor no •m firai; | Never again shall I trust them; |
| C'aissi com las solh chaptener, | As much as I was formerly their protector |
| Enaissi las deschaptenrai: | I shall now neglect them: |
| Pois vei c'una pro no m'en te | Since no woman will come to my aid |
| Vas leis que •m destrui e •m cofon, | With her who destroys and confounds me |
| Totas las dopt e las mescre, | I fear them all and mistrust them |
| Car be sai c'atretals se son. | For well I know that they are all alike. |

| | |
|---|---|
| D'aisso •s fa be femma parer | May lady wants to appear a good woman; |
| Ma domna, per qu'e •lh o retrai, | So I discourage her; |
| Car no vol so c'om deu voler, | For she does not want what she should, |
| E so com li deveda, fai. | And what is forbidden her, she does. |
| Chazutz sui en mala merce, | I have fallen into disfavor |
| Et ai be faih co •l fols en pon; | And behaved like the fool on the bridge |
| E no sai per que m'esdeve | And I do not know how it came about |
| Mas car trop puyei contra mon. | Unless it was that I applied too much pressure. |

| | |
|---|---|
| Merces es perduda, per ver, | Mercy is lost, truly |
| (Et eu non o saubi anc mai), | (And I never knew it) |
| Car cilh qui plus en degr' aver, | For she who should have had most |
| No •n a ges; et on la querrai? | Has none: and where should I seek it now? |
| A! can mal sembla qui la ve, | Oh! how pitiful it seems to him who sees— |
| Que aquest chaitiu deziron | Wretched and lovesick as I am, |
| Que ja ses leis non aura be, | Unable to know happiness without her— |
| Laisse morir, que no l'aon! | How she lets me die, and will not come to my aid. |

| | |
|---|---|
| Pus ab midons no •m pot valer | Since nothing can help me with my lady, |
| Precs ni merces ni •l dreihz qu'eu ai | Neither prayers nor grace, nor the rights that I have, |
| Ni a leis no ven a plazer | Since it does not please her that I love her |
| Qu'eu l'am, ja mais no •lh o dirai. | I shall not speak of my love again. |
| Aissi •m part d'amor e •m recre: | I give up my love and deny it; |
| Mort m'a, e per mort li respon, | She has willed my death, and I answer it with death; |
| E vau m'en, pus ilh no •m rete, | I leave, since she does not hold me back, |
| Chaitus, en issilh, no sai on. | And go wretched into exile, not knowing where. |

| | |
|---|---|
| Tristeza no •n auretz de me, | You will not see my sorrow, |
| Qu'eu m'en vau, chaitius, no sai on. | Since I am going, wretched, not knowing where. |
| De chantar me gic e •m recre, | I renounce and deny my songs |
| E de joi e d'amor m'escon. | And flee from joy and from love. |

# DE BONE AMOR

TROUVERE CHANSON

*GACE BRULÉ*

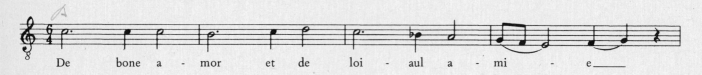

De bone a - mor et de loi - aul a - mi - e __

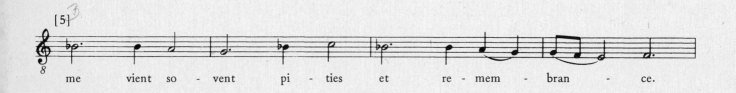

[5] me vient so - vent pi - ties et re - mem - bran - ce.

[10] Si ke ja maix, a nul jour de ma vi - e, __ n'o - bli - er -

[15] ai ces jeuls ne sa sem - blan - ce. Por ceu s'A - mors ne s'en

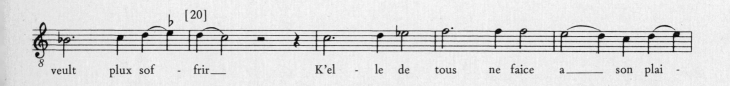

[20] veult plux sof - frir __ K'el - le de tous ne faice a __ son plai -

[25] xir __ et de tou - tes, __ maix ne puet a - ven - ir __

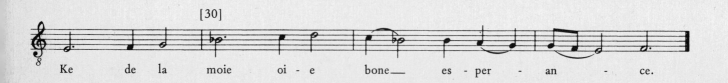

[30] Ke de la moie oi - e bone __ es - per - an - ce.

28

Of good love and of (my) loyal (lady) friend
Compassion and memories often come to me
In such a way that not one day of my life
Shall I forget her face or the way she looks.
For this reason, if Love will not be willing to refrain
From doing with all men as she pleases,
And all women, it can never happen
That my love will have high hope.

## II

Coment poroie avoir bone
    *esperance*
A bone Amor et a leal amie,
Ne a biauz yeuz, n'a la douce
    semblance
Que ne verrai jamès jor de ma vie?
Amer m'estuet, ne m'en puis plus
    soffrir,
Celi cui ja ne vanra a plaisir.
Siens sui, coment qu'il m'en doie
    avenir,
Et si n'i voi ne confort ne *ahie*.

How could I have high
    hope
For good love and a loyal friend,
Neither beautiful eyes nor sweet
    countenance
Will I ever see one day in my life?
I must love, though I can hardly endure it any
    longer
One whom my love never pleases.
I am hers, whatever may happen
    to me,
Even though I see neither comfort from her nor help.

## III

Coment avrai je confort ne *ahie*
Encontre Amour vers cui nuns n'a
    puissance?
Amer me fait ce qui ne m'ainme
    mie,
Donc ja n'avrai fors ennui et
    pesance.
Ne ja nul jor ne l'oserai gehir,
Celi qui tant de max me fait sentir.
Mais de tel mort sui jugiez a morir
Dont ja ne quier veoir ma *delivrance*.

How could I get comfort or help
Against Love, over which no one has
    power?
Love makes me love the one who does not
    love me
Thus I will have nothing but sorrow and
    chagrin
Neither now nor ever will I dare to confess my love
To the one who makes me feel so much pain.
For I am condemned to die such a death
From which I do not seek deliverance.

## IV

Je ne vois pas querant tel *delivrance*
Par quoi amors soit de moi
    departie;
Ne ja n'en quier nul jor avoir
    poissance,
Ainz vuil amer ce qui ne n'ainme
    mie.
N'il n'est pas droiz; je li doie gehir.
Por nul destroit que me face sentir
N'avrai confort; n'i voi que dou
    morir,
Puis que je voi que *ne m'ameroit mie*.

I do not seek such deliverance
Through which love would leave
    me;
I never seek to have this
    power,
Rather, I want to love the one who does not
    love me
It is not right that I should confess to her.
No matter what torment that she might make me feel
I will not gain comfort: I see only sweet
    death
Since I know that she would not love me.

## V

Ne m'ameroit? Ice ne sai je *mie,*
Que fins amis doit par bone
    atendance
Et par soffrir conquerre tel amie.
Mes je n'i puis avoir bone fiance,
Que cele est tex por cui plaing et
    sopir
Que ma dolor ne doigneroit oir.
Si me vaut mienz garder mon bon
    taisir
Que dire riens qui li tort a *grevance*

Would she not love me? This I don't know,
For a tender friend must, by patient
    waiting
And by suffering, conquer such a lady friend.
I can never be completely certain
Since she is one—this one for whom
    I lament and sigh—
Who would not deign to listen to my sorrow.
Thus it is better for me to maintain my good
    silence
Than to say anything which she would take as
    an annoyance.

## VI

Ne vos doit pas trop torner a
    grevance.
Se je vos aing, dame, plus que ma
    vie
Que c'est la riens ou j'ai greignor
    fiance,
Que, par moi seul vos os nommer
    amie
Et por ce fais maint dolorous sopir,
Qu'assez vos puis et veoir et oir.
Mais, quant vos voi, n'i a que dou
    taisir.
Que si sui pris que ne sai que
    je die.

It must not cause you such
    annoyance
If I love you, milady, more than my life
Because the dream in which I have the
    greatest faith
Is that I alone shall dare to call you
    my beloved
And for this I make many painful sighs
For I am not able to see you or hear you.
But, when I see you, there is only sweet
    silence
Because I am overwhelmed and don't know
    what I am saying.

## VII

Hé Clemondoz! que ferai je
    d'amie
Quant je avrai trespassée
    m'enfance?
Et ma dame qui si ert envoisie
Avra dou tout lessié l'aler en dance?
Lors dira l'en: "Soffriz, sire,
    soffriz."
Lors, mal a tens, me vient au
    repentir
C'il soffre trop qui laisse autrui joir
De ce dont a traite la penitance.

Mes biaus conforz ne m'en porra
    garir;
De vos amer ne me porrai partir,
N'a vos parler, ne ne m'en puis
    taisir
Que mon mal trait en chantant ne
    vos die.

Par Deu, Huet, ne m'en puis [plus]
    soffrir
Qu'en Bertree est et ma morz et
    ma vie.

Hey, forgiving God! what shall I do with my
    beloved
When I have outgrown my youth?
And my lady, who will be so joyous,
Will she at last be allowed to dance?
Then people will say "Suffer, sire,
    suffer"
So, at the wrong time, I repent.
He suffers too much who lets others enjoy
That which deserves punishment.

My beautiful dream will not be able
    to cure me;
I will not be able to save myself from loving you,
Nor from speaking to you, I cannot be silent
About my pain; cannot keep, as I sing,
    from telling you.

God almighty, Huet, I can no longer
    endure it
For in Bertree is my death and my
    life.

# BLÔZEN WIR DEN ANGER LIGEN SÂHEN (minnesinger)

MINNELIED

NEIDHART VON REUENTAL

Blôzen wir den anger ligen sahen, end uns diu liebe zit begunde nahen, daz die bluomen drungen durch den kle aber als e. heide diust mit rosen nu bevangen: den tuot der sumer wol, niht we.

Droschel, nahtigal die hoert man singen, von ir schalle berc unt tal erklingen: si vreunt sich gegen der lieben sumerzit, diu uns git vreuden vil und liehter ougenweide. diu heide wünneclichen lit.

Sprach ein maget: „die wisen wellent touwen. megt ir an dem sumer wunder schouwen? die boume, die den winder stuonden val, über al sint si niuwes loubes worden riche: dar under singent nahtigal.

Bare was the meadow when we looked at it until that lovely time approached when the flowers pierced through the clover, as ever. Now the heath is lined with roses: the summer does them good, not harm.

One can hear thrushes and nightingales sing; from their song mountains and valleys resound: they rejoice over the lovely summertime, which gives us much happiness and feasts our eyes. Wonderfully lies the heath.

Said a maiden: "The meadows will thaw. Can you see the marvels of summer? The trees, bare during the winter, are now abundant with new leaves and the nightingales sing in their branches.

31

Losa, wie die vogele alle doenent, wie si den meien mit ir sange kroenent! ja, waen ich, der winder ende hat. Wierat, sprinc also, daz ich dirs immer danke! diu linde wol geloubet stat.

Da sul wir uns wider hiuwer zweien. vor dem walde ist rosen vil geheien: der wil ich ein kränzel wolgetan ufe han, springe ich einem ritter an der hende in hohem muote. nu wol dan!"

,,Tohterlin, la dich sin niht gelangen! wil du die ritter an dem reien drangen, die dir niht ze maze ensulen sin, tohterlin, du wirst an dem schaden wol ervunden. der junge meier muotet din.''

,,Sliezet mir den meier an die versen! ja truwe ich stolzem ritter wol gehersen: zwiu sol ein gebuwer mir ze man? der enkan mich nach minem willen niht getriuten: er, waen, min eine muoz gestan.''

,,Tohterlin, la dir in niht versmahen! du wilt ze tumbe ritters künde vahen: daz ist allen dinen vriunden leit. manegen eit swüere du: des wis nu ane lougen, din muot dich allez von mir treit!''

,,Muoter min, ir lazet iuwer bagen! ich wil mine vriunde durch in wagen, den ich minen willen nie verhal. über al müezen sin die liute werden inne: min muot der strebt gein Riuwental.''

Listen, how the birds burst into song, crowning May with their voices; yes, I believe winter has come to an end. Maiden Wierat, spring and dance, so that I may always thank you for it! The linden stands there full of leaves.

There we should come together again. In front of the forest many roses have grown. From them I will wear a well-made little chaplet when dancing with pride at the hand of a knight. Well then!

"Young daughter, do not long for a knight. Will you throng among knights in the round-dance? They are not for you, young daughter, for you will soon suffer harm. The young Meier wants you."

"Take that Meier out of my way! I can well have a proud young knight for company; how could I get along with a peasant as a husband? He could not caress me as I would like; he will have to be without me."

"Young daughter, do not disdain him! How stupid to want a knight! All your friends are sorry about that. You have often sworn not to do it. Keep to your promise now! Otherwise your wantonness will take you from me!"

"Stop your scolding, mother mine, for him I will put my friends to the test. I have never concealed my intention to them. Everywhere people shall know: My being tends towards Reuental."

Take care that no one looks at me;
If anyone should look at me, warn me at once.
It is all down there in those woods.
Take care that no one looks at me.
The country girl tends her cows.
"Pretty brunette, I am yours."
Take care that no one looks at me;
If anyone should look at me, warn me at once.

# PRENDÉS I GARDE

RONDEAU

GUILLAUME D'AMIENS

Prendés i garde, s'on mi regarde!

[5] S'on mi regarde, dites le moi.

[10] C'est tout la jus en cel boschaige;

Prendés i garde, s'on mi regarde. [15]

La pastourele i garde vaches: [20]

Plaisans brunete a vous m'otroil,

[25] Prendés i garde, s'on mi regarde!

[30] S'on mi regarde, dites le moi.

# LAS CANTIGAS DE SANTA MARIA

PROLOGO

ALFONSO EL SABIO

Por - que tro - bar é cou - sa en que jaz en - ten - di -
men - to, por - en quen o faz á - o d'a - ver, et de ra - zon as - saz,
per - que en - ten - da et sa - bia di - zer o que en - tend' e de
di - zer lie praz; ca ben tro - bar as - si s'á de ffa - zer.

[Este é o prologo das Cantigas de Santa Maria, eimentando as cousas que á mester en o trobar.]

[This is the Prologue to the Songs of Holy Mary, indicating which qualities are important for writing verse.]

Since writing verse is an art
which entails deep understanding,
a troubadour, therefore, must have sufficient
   knowledge
to understand and express what he feels
and wishes to say.
Good verse is made this way.

E macar eu estas duas non ey
com' eu querria, pero provarei
a mostrar ende un pouco que sei,
confiand' en Deus, ond' o saber ven,
ca per ele tenno que poderei
mostrar do que quero algua ren.

Though I do not understand as much
as I would wish, still I will try
to show the little that I perceive,
trusting in God, the source of all we know,
from Whom I have whatever I may
reveal of the troubadour's art.

Des o - ge mais quer eu tro - bar pol - a Se - nnor on - rra - da, en que Deus quis_ car - ne_ fi - llar, bẽ - ey - ta et_ sa - gra - da, por nos_ dar gran sol - da - da no seu rey - no_ et nos_ er - dar por seus de sa mas - na - da de vi - da per - lon - ga - da, sen a - ver - mos pois a pas - sar per mort' ou - tra ve - ga - da.

[Esta é a primeira cantiga de loor de Santa Maria ementando os VII goyos que ouve de seu Fillo].

[This is the first song of praise to Holy Mary, mentioning the Seven Joys she received from her Son.]

From now on I will be troubadour of that
    noble Lady
in whom God took mortal flesh now sanctified
    and holy,
to bestow the inheritance of eternal life
and grant us a place in His kingdom
ever free from the pain of death.

E poren quero comecar como foy
    saudada
de Gabriel, u lle chamar foy: "Ben
aventurada Virgen, de Deus amada,
do que o mund' a de salvar ficas ora
    prennada;
e demais ta cunnada
Elisabeth, que foi dultar, e end'
envergonnada"

And thus I wish to begin as you were
    greeted
by Gabriel, he said to you: "Favored Virgin,
beloved of God,
be now filled with Him who will save
    the world;
and now your cousin
Elizabeth, who once despaired, is repen-
    tant and great with child"

# VIDERUNT HEMANUEL

ST. MARTIAL MELISMATIC ORGANUM

*ANONYMOUS*

All the ends of the earth have seen Emanuel, the only-begotten Son of the Father, offered for the fall and for the salvation of Israel, man created in time, word in the beginning, born in the palace of the city which he had founded, the salvation of our God. Be joyful in the Lord, all ye lands.

# VIDERUNT OMNES

NOTRE DAME ORGANUM

*LEONIN*

[30]

[35]

om -

[40]

[45]

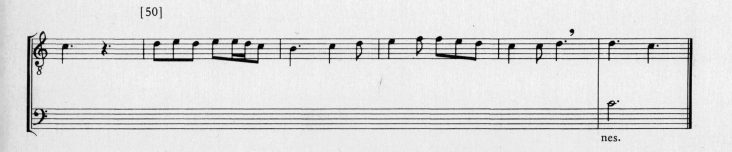

[50]

nes.

38  *Leonin*

# VIDERUNT OMNES

ORGANUM QUADRUPLUM

*PEROTIN*

13. ru - bus ru - bet ig - ne 14. vi - rens in ru - bo - re. 15. vir - ga ver - nat flo - re,

16. vir - go no - vo mo - re 17. pa - rit cum pu - do - re. 18. So - lem sy - de - re

DE -

DE -

19. pro - ce - de - re. ful - ge - re VI - DE 21. sy - dus sin - gu - la - re, 22. tu - um SA - LU - TA - RE.

20.

DE -

23. Stel - le sig - no ful - gi - de quod ra - di - at hoc ma - re, 25. ar - ri - de, con - fi - de,

24.

39. De - um iux - ta bru - tum, 40. an - gu - lo, sac - cu - lo, 41. re - gem in - vo - lu - tum.

42. Re - sti - tu - tum 43. pa - ter par - vu - lum 44. ce - so gau - det vi - tu - lo,

45. cum os - cu - lo 46. dat a - nu - lum. 47. Lu - to spu - tum, 48. spu - to lu - tum

49. et u - ni - tum et li - ni - tum, cu - i sa - nat ocu - lum, 52. sta - tum da - tum 53. post

42  *Anonymous*

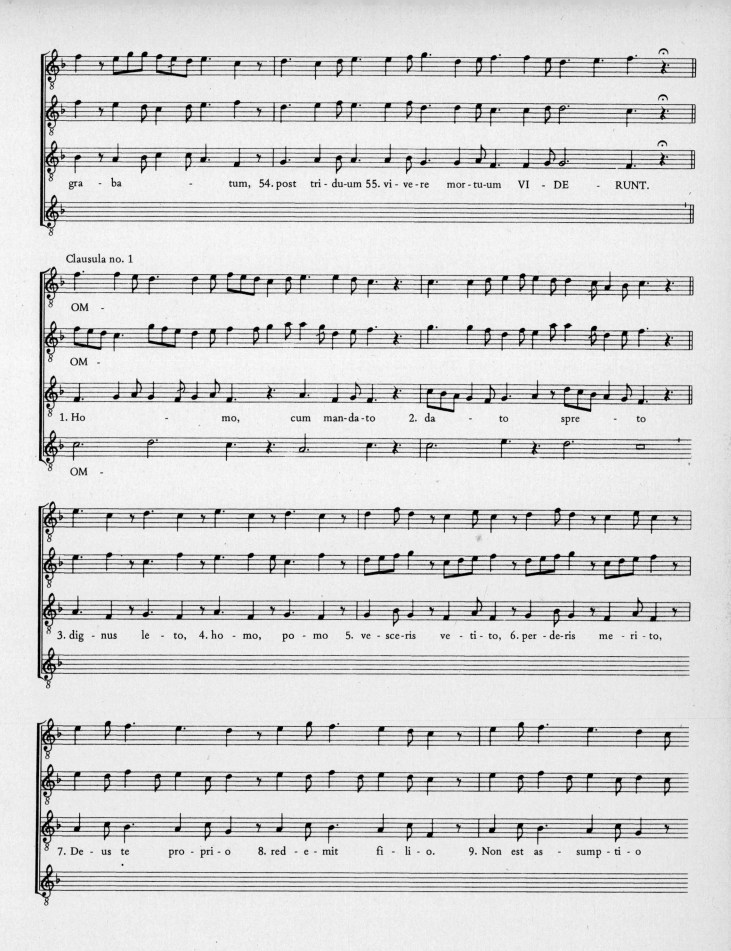

gra - ba - - tum, 54. post tri-du-um 55. vi-ve-re mor-tu-um VI - DE - RUNT.

Clausula no. 1

OM -

OM -

1. Ho - mo, cum man-da-to 2. da - to spre - to

OM -

3. dig - nus le - to, 4. ho - mo, po - mo 5. ve-sce-ris ve - ti-to, 6. per-de-ris me - ri-to,

7. De - us te pro-pri-o 8. red-e-mit fi-li-o. 9. Non est as - sump-ti-o

10. De - i con - sump - ti - o 11. car - nis in con - iu - gi - o 12. ver - bi. Ma - net vi - ti - o

13. tu - a re - for - ma - ti - o, 14. ta - lis ut for - ma - ti - o, 15. quan - do pri - mo nup - sit li - mo. 16.

17. Spi - ri - tus con - iunc - ti - o 18. lu - to fit u - ni - to spu - to, 19. 20. ce - co li - to

21. re - pa - ra - ta vi - si - o, 22. tu - a re - pa - ra - ti - o. 23. Lu - tum com - ma - du - it

44  *Anonymous*

24. spu - ti co - nu - bi - o, 25. spu - tum non vi - lu - it 26. lu - ti con - sor - ti - o,

27. neu - trum ab - sor - bu - it 28. is - ta con - mix - ti - o. 29. Sal - vat, quas mis - cu - it

30. na - tu - ras, u - ni - o 31. OM

NES
NES
NES.
NES

fi - nes ter - rae sa - lu - ta - re

De - i nos - tri: ju - bi - la - te De - o

o - mnis ter - ra.

# EXCITATUR CARITAS IN YERICO

CONDUCTUS

ANONYMOUS

Ex - ci - ta - tur ca - ri - tas in Ye - ri - co. Fac - ta est plu -

Ex - ci - ta - tur ca - ri - tas in Ye - ri - co. Fac - ta est plu -

[5]

ra - li - tas in u - ni - co. Ja - cob ex - u - lat, et pul - lu -

ra - li - tas in u - ni - co. Ja - cob ex - u - lat, et pul - lu -

[10]

lat fi - des in gen - ti - bus. La - pis tol - li - tur, fons o - ri -

lat fi - des in gen - ti - bus. La - pis tol - li - tur, fons o - ri -

46

Let charity be aroused in Jericho
Many sacrifices have been made into one.
Jacob exults and faith sprouts up among the people.
The rock is lifted, fountains rise giving drink to the flocks.
The Son of God, none other, has lifted up man.
The Divine Spirit has showered down his blessings on the Virgin.

# THIRTEENTH CENTURY MOTETS

TANT ME PLAIST/TOUT LI CUERS/OMNES

*ANONYMOUS*

Triplum: Tant_____ me plaist a vos pen-ser, Fins cuers a-mou-

Duplum: Tout li cuers me rit de joi-e De vos-tre biau-te ve-

Tenor: OMNES

[5]

rous et doz, Ce qui me so-vient de vos Et me fet ce

ir; Mes ce qu'il m'es-tuet par-tir De vous, plei-sant, simple et

[10]

chant trou-ver, Pour la do-lour o-bli-er

coi-e, Et a-lor es-tran-ge voi-e,

[15]

Que je sent au de - par - tir; Ne con - fort n'en voi ve - nir,

Fet ma joie en duel ver - tir; Ne ja ne m'em puis souf - frir. Que

Dieus, las! fors sam plus del so - ve - nir Que chan -

je ne voi - se si vos proi; Por Diu! ne m'ou -

[20]

ter a hau - te vois Vos o - i a ma de - vi - se: *Dieus!*

bli - es mi - e, Se plus so - vent ne vos voi. Las! je m'en

[25]

*Par ci va la mi - gno - ti - se, Par ci ou je vois.*

vois, ma douce a - mi - e, Si vous lais, ce poi - se moi.

It pleases me so much to think of you,
Delicate heart, loving and tender,
The reason I remember you
And which causes me to create this song
Is to forget the pain
Which I felt at the moment when we parted.

Ne confort n'en voi venir,
Dieus, las! fors sam plus del sovenir
Que chanter a haute vois
Vos o'i a ma devise:
*Dieus! Par ce va la mignotise,*
*Par ce ou je vois.*

I see no comfort coming
God, alas! with nothing more than memories
I sing aloud
Then I hear you (saying) upon my departure:
God! That is why gallantry goes
Wherever I go.

*Duplum:*

Tout li cuers me rit de joie
De vostre biauté veir
Mes ce qu'il m'estuet partir
De vous, pleisant, simple et coie,
Et aler estrange voie,
Fet ma joie en duel vertir;

My whole heart laughs with joy
To see your beauty
But that which makes me leave
You, pleasant, simple and quiet (one),
And go away on a strange journey,
Makes my joy turn into mourning.

Ne ja ne m'empuis souffrir.
Que je ne voise si vos proi;
Por Diu! ne m'oublies mie,
Se plus sovent ne vos voi.
Las! je m'en vois, ma douce amie,
Si vous lais, ce poise moi.

Neither now nor later do I want to suffer
From lack of seeing you, so I pray of you
For God's sake, don't forget me
In case I never see you again.
Alas! I am going away, my sweet friend,
My leaving you weighs (heavily) on me.

**50 Anonymous**

Dieus! ou pour-rai je trou-ver Mer - ci,                    Quant n'os

Ce sont a - mou - re-tes qui mi tien - nent si

OMNES

di - re mon pan - ser   A ce - li   Qui par

Que ne pans a riens vi - vant   Fors qu'a la bele

sa biau - té   A mon cuer ra - vi   Et en -

au cler vis. A, mi!   Sa blan - che gorge et plai -

pri - son - né? He, las! si mar la vi,   Quant je

sans, Son men - ton vou - tis,   Sa sa - fre bou -

52 *Anonymous*

mours es - pris Et si sou - pris Que par mes ieus
brun sour - cill plai - sant, Son plain front, son chief lui -

[55] [60]
sui tra - his, Ce m'est a - vis. Vous qui la i - rez,
sant M'ont na - vré D'un dart si en - a - mou -

[65]
pour Dieu, di - tes li: "Dou - ce de - si - ree au
ré Que bien croi que m'o - ci - ra. Ha, dieus,

[70]
cuer jo - li, Car a - ies pi - tié de vostre a - mi."
ha! Ha, dieus, ha! Ha - ro, qui m'en ga - ri - ra?

Dieus! ou pourrai je trouver Merci,
Quant n'os dire mon panser
A celi
Qui par sa biauté
A mon cuer ravi
Et enprisonné?
He, las! si mar la vi,
Quant je n'ai pensee fors qu'a li!
Quant je remir sa bouchete
Et la coulour de son cler vis
Et sa polie gorgete
Plaisant et blanchete
Plus que flour de lis:
Lors sui si d'amours espris
Et si soupris
Qui par mes ieus sui trahis,
Ce m'est avis.
Vous qui la irez,
Pour Dieu, dites li:
"Douce desiree au cuer joli,
Car aiés pitié de vostre ami."

God! Where will I be able to find mercy
When I dare not say what I think
To the one
Who, by her beauty,
Has ravished my heart
And imprisoned it?
Ah, alas! So afflicting (is) life
When I have thought only about her
When I look at her little mouth
And the color of her fair face
And her graceful little throat
Pleasing and white
More than a fleur de lys:
At that time I am so taken with love
And so surprised
That I am betrayed by my eyes,
It seems to me.
You, who will go to her,
For God's sake, tell her:
"Sweet object of desire with a pretty heart
Have mercy on your friend."

*Duplum:*

Ce sont amouretes qui me tiennent si
Que ne pans ariens vivant
Fors qu'a la bele au cler vis.
A, mi!
Sa blanche gorge et plaisans,
Son menton voutis,
Sa safre bouche riant.
Qui tous jours dit par semblant:
"Baisiés, baisiés moi, amis, Tous dis,"
Son nes bien fait a devis
Et si vair oell fremiant,
Larron d'anbler cuer d'amant
Et si brun sourcill plaisant,
Son plain front, son chief luisant
M'ont navré
D'un dart si enamouré
Que bien croi que m'ocira
Ha dieus, ha!
Ha dieus, ha!
Haro, qui m'en garira?

It is my love which holds me in such a way
That I think of nothing alive
Except the beautiful (lady) with a clear face.
Ah, me!
Her white and pleasant throat,
Her curved chin
Her laughing mouth like a sapphire.
Which, every day, seems to say:
"Kiss me, kiss me, friend. All of you I say."
Her nose pleasingly well made
And her shining eyes sparkling,
Thief of stolen lover's heart
And such pleasing brown brow,
Her smooth forehead, her shining head
Have wounded me
With an arrow so full of love
That I really think it will kill me
Ha, God, ha!
Ha, God, ha!
Help! Who will cure me?

Triplum: Se je sui lies et chan - tans, C'est de rai - son, Car bele et bone et sa - chans M'en done o - choi - son, Par uns ieus vairs et ri - ans, Hou - neur pro - me - tans, Et le no - ble guer - re - don Des fius a - mans. Et si croi com voir di - sans Qu'en si - cle n'en re - li - gi - on N'est pe - tis ne grans,

Duplum: Jo - li - e - te - ment, De cuer bo - ne - ment, Au dou - cet de cors gent M'est a - vis que ren -

Tenor: OMNES

Se je sui lies et chantans,
C'est de raison,
Car bele et bone et sachans
M'en done ochoison,
Par uns ieus vairs et rians,
Houneur prometans,
Et le noble guerredon
Des flus amans.
Et si croi com voir disans
Qu'en sicle n'en religion
N'est petis ne grans,
Pour qu'il soit bien connoissans,
Que pour si bele fachon
Ne levast le chaperon,
Et qu'il ne vaus ist tons tans
Estre de tout a li obeisans;
Et quant dame de telnon,
Si tres noble et si poissans,
Si sade et si deduisans
Et si avenans,
A moi, qui de discrecion
Et de sens et de renon
Sui ou nombre des enfans,
A doné si noble don,
Que ses regars atraians
Me promet le grant foison
De grans deduis dont je sui desirans,
Bien i doi estre enclinans
Et faire chanson,
Car biauté a plus cent ans

Que ne dit *cief bien seans.*

If I should be happy and composing a song
It is with good reason,
For a lady, beautiful, good and well-bred
Gives me cause for it,
With her shining, laughing eyes,
Promising virtue,
And the noble reward
Of the chosen lover.
And thus I believe what the truth says
That neither in riches nor in religion
Is there (a man) small or great,
Who is so knowledgeable
That, for such a beautiful face
Would not doff his hat,
And this is worth a lifetime
To be in all ways obedient to her;
And when a lady of such renown
So very noble and so powerful,
So gracious and so charming
And so appealing,
To me, who, in wisdom
And in reason and in renown
Is among the children,
Has given such noble gift
That her alluring glances at me
Promise me an abundance
Of great pleasures, which I so desire,
I must indeed submit
And create a song,
Because if beauty (must wait) more than a
   hundred years
It can no longer be addressed in an accept-
   able manner.

Jolietement,
De cuer bonement,
Au doucet de cors gent
M'est avis que rendue
Me sui comme loial drue,
Si que mise outréement
Sans estre esperdue
Me sui en amour sagement,
Car par mon ami n'ier ja deceue,
Ains m'amera de tout entierement.

Happily,
With a heart full of pleasure,
To the sweetness of a beautiful body
It seems to me that I submitted
Like a loyal mistress,
In such a way that I was without restraint.
Without being desperate
I became learned in the matters of love,
For I will never be deceived by my friend,
Rather he will love me completely.

60 *Anonymous*

*Triplum:*

S'on me regarde,
S'on me regarde,
Dites le moi;
Trop sui gaillarde,
Bien l'aperchoi.
Ne puis laissier que mon regard ne s'esparde,
Car tes m'esgarde
Dont mout me tarde
Qu'il m'ait o soi,
Qu'il a en foi,
De m'amour plain otroi;
Mais tel ce voi
Qui est, je croi,
Feu d'enfer l'arde!
Jalous de moi.
Mais pour li d'amer ne recroi,
Car par ma foi
Pour nient m'esgarde,
Bien pert sa garde:
J'arai rechoi.

If anyone looks at me,
If anyone looks at me,
Please tell me:
I am too much a wench.
As I well know.
I just cannot help having wandering eyes.
There is one man
Who looks at me
With whom I yearn to be.
Because he is the one
Who enjoys all my love:
But here I see a man
who is, I think,
—may he burn in hell!—
jealous of me.
But not for him will I give up my love,
For, believe me,
There is no point in his watching me,
Since I know what he is up to:
I swear I'll find a secret place.

*Duplum:*

Prennés i garde, S'on me regarde;
Trop sui gaillarde,
Dites le moi,
Pour Dieu vous proi,
Car tes m'esgarde
Dont mout me tarde
Qu'il m'ait o soi
Bien l'aperchoi,
Et tel chi voi
Qui est, je croi,
Feu d'enfer l'arde!
Jalous de moi.
Mais pour li d'amer ne recroi,
Pour nient m'esgarde,
Bien pert sa garde:
J'arai rechoi,
Et de mon amie dosnoi.
Faire le doi,
Ne serai plus couarde.

Take care, if anyone looks at me
I am too much a wench,
Please tell me,
For God's sake I beg of you,
There is one man
Who looks at me
With whom I yearn to be
As I well know,
And another I see here
Who is, I think,
—may he burn in hell!—
jealous of me.
But not for him will I give up my love,
There is no point in his watching me,
Since I know what he is up to:
I shall find a secret place,
And pleasure with my lover.
I must do it,
No longer shall I be a coward.

*Tenor:*

Hé! mi enfant

Oh! my children!

# PROMESSES/HA! FORTUNE/ET NON EST

GUILLAUME DE MACHAUT

ISORHYTHMIC

62

64  *Guillaume de Machaut*

*Triplum:* Whoever puts faith in Fortune's promises, secures himself in the riches of its gifts, and believes Fortune is a friend — is a fool, for Fortune is not reliable. Without faith, law, justice, or moderation, Fortune is refuse, richly clothed and glistening without, but foul within. An idol of false countenance in which no one must believe and from which no one can expect aid. Its appearance of virtue is but wind and whatever it represents can be nothing but false. Its victims are always in danger of stumbling, since by its false nature, the disloyal one reneges and is false, treacherous, perverse, and a bitter mother. Blessed and then pierced by a mortal thrust are those who nourish themselves on Fortune and are then destroyed by treason.

*Motetus:* Fortune! you have put me at sea far from port. I am helpless in a small, flat boat without a sail. All about are unfavorable winds intent on my destruction so that there is neither comfort nor protection. There is neither mercy, escape, nor salvation for me. Without just cause a bitter and unfair death stands ready to destroy me. And this death I receive, false Fortune, through your machinations and treachery.

*Tenor:* And there is none to help.

# HONTE, PAOUR, DOUBTANCE

BALLADE

GUILLAUME DE MACHAUT

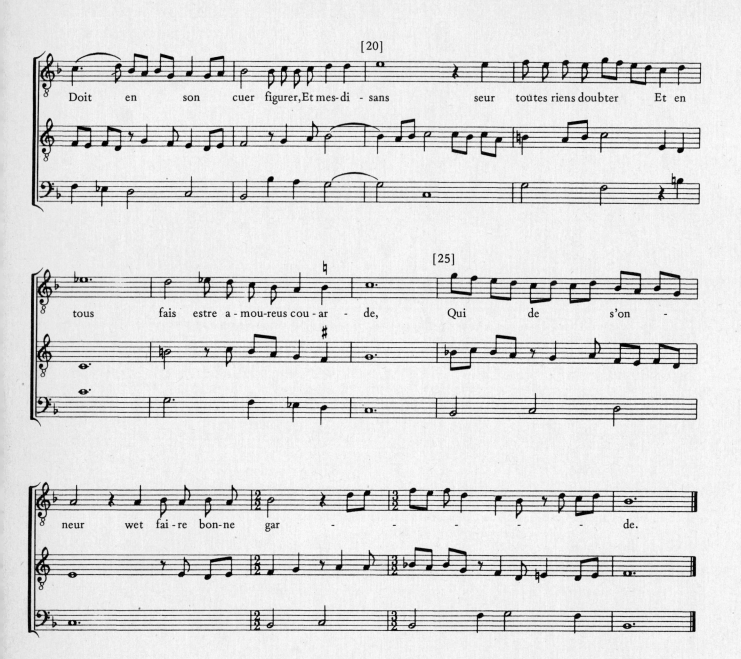

Doit en son cuer figurer, Et mes-di - sans seur toutes riens doubter Et en

tous fais estre a - mou-reus cou - ar - de, Qui de s'on -

neur wet fai - re bon-ne gar - - - - - de.

Shame, fright, fear of wrong doing
Moderation in her desire
Big in refusal and slow in giving
Reason, measure, honor, and honesty
She must show in her heart
And fear the wrong saying of all things
And in all occasions be a fearful lover
The lady who wants to protect her honor.

Sage en maintieng, au bien penre
    exemplaire,
Celer a point s'amour et son secre,

Wise in behavior, she follows the good as
    example
She hides the smallest manifestation of her
    love and secret

Simple d'atour et non vouloir attraire

Simple in her attire, she does not want to
    attract attention

Pluseurs a li par samblant d'amitie,
Car c'est pour amans tuer;
Foy, pais, amour et loyaute garder,
Ce sont les poins que dame en son cuer
    garde,
Qui de s'onneur wet faire bonne garde.

She pretends to like several others
To upset her lover
She must keep faith, country, love and loyalty
These are the points that the lady keeps in
    her heart
The lady who wants to protect her honor.

Quar quant amour maint en cuer
    debonnaire,
Jone, gentil, de franchise paré,
Plain de cuidier et de joieus afaire
Et de desir par plaisence engenré,
C'est trop fort a contrester,
Qu'il font souvent senz et mesure
    outrer;
Pour ce ades pense a ces poins et
    resgarde
Qui de s'onneur wet faire bonne garde.

For when love inhabits a well-bred
    heart
Young, sweet, adorned with frankness
Full of feelings, of happy disposition
And of desire born of pleasure
It is so hard to resist
That they often exceed good sense and
    measure
For that reason she thinks unceasingly about
    these points and reflects attentively
The lady who wants to protect her honor.

# DOUCE DAME JOLIE

VIRELAI

GUILLAUME DE MACHAUT

R 1.5.Dou - ce da - me jo - li - e, Pour Dieu ne pen - ses
4.He - las! et je men - di - e D'es - pe - rance et d'a-

mi - e Que nulle ait sig - nou - ri - e Seur moy fors vous seu - le - ment.
i - e; Dont ma joie est fe - ni - e, Se pi - te ne vous en prent.

2. Qu'a - des sans tri - che - ri - e Chie - ri - e Vous
3. Tous les jours de ma vi - e Ser - vi - e Sans

1.
ay et hum - ble - ment
2.
vi - lein pen - se - ment.

| | |
|---|---|
| Douce dame jolie, | Sweet lovely lady, |
| Pour Dieu ne penses mie | For the love of God, do not suppose |
| Que nulle ait signourie | That anyone has dominion |
| Seur moy fors vous seulement. | Over me but you alone. |
| | |
| Qu'ades sans tricherie | You have I ever without guile |
| Chierie | Cherished |
| Vous ay et humblement | And humbly |
| Tous les jours de ma vie | All the days of my life |
| Servie | Served |
| Sans vilein pensement. | With no ignoble thought. |
| Helas! Et je mendie | Alas! I am deprived |
| D'esperance et d'aie; | Of hope and help; |
| Dont ma joie est fenie, | For my joy is ended |
| Se pite ne vous en prent. | If you have no pity. |
| | |
| Douce dame jolie, etc. | Sweet lovely lady, etc. |
| | |
| Mais vo douce maistrie | But your sweet mastery |
| Maistrie | Masters |
| Mon cuer si durement | My heart so severely |
| Qu'elle le contralie | That my heart is tormented |
| Et lie | And bound |
| En amours tellement | So much in love |
| Qu'il n'a de riens envie | That it has no desire |
| Fors d'estre en vo baillie; | Except to be in your keeping; |
| Et se ne lie ottrie | And yet it is not granted |
| Vos cuers nul aligement. | By your heart any relief. |
| | |
| Douce dame jolie, etc. | Sweet lovely lady, etc. |

| | |
|---|---|
| Et quant ma maladie | And since my malady |
| Garie | Cured |
| Ne sera nullement | Will never be |
| Sans vous, douce anemie, | Without you, sweet enemy, |
| Qui lie | Who rejoice |
| Estes de mon tourment, | In my torment, |
| A jointes mains deprie | With joined hands I beseech |
| Vo cuer, puis qu'il m'oublie, | Your heart, since it ignores me, |
| Que temprement m'ocie, | That it shortly kill me, |
| Car trop langui longuement. | For I have too long languished. |
| | |
| Douce dame jolie, etc. | Sweet lovely lady, etc. |

# ROSE, LIZ, PRINTEMPS, VERDURE

RONDEAU

GUILLAUME DE MACHAUT

1-2. 6-7. 11-12. Ro - se,            liz,
4-5. Et tous          les
8-9. Et quant         tou

prin - temps, ver - du - re,        Fleur,
biens de Na - tu - re,             A -
te cre - a - tu - re             Seur -

bau - me
vez
mon

The rose, the lily, the springtime and greenery,
The flower, balm and the sweetest of perfumes,
You surpass them all, my love, in sweetness.

And you possess all Nature's gifts,
Wherefore I adore you.

The rose, the lily, the springtime and greenery,
The flower, balm and the sweetest of perfumes.

And were every creature
To exceed your worth,
Yet may I say and truly:

The rose, the lily, the springtime and greenery,
The flower, balm and the sweetest of perfumes,
You surpass them all, my love, in sweetness.

# ENICE FU'

MADRIGAL

JACOPO DA BOLOGNA

I was a phoenix pure and soft, and now I have been changed into a turtle dove that flies with love through the beautiful garden. Neither the parched tree nor the muddy water delights me. Because of this I am in a quandary. The summer is going and winter will soon follow. Thus have I lived, still live, and can write that no gift is of more value than to live virtuously.

# CHON BRACHI ASSAI

CACCIA

*GIOVANNI DA FIRENZE*

Ritornello

So - lae - - ra li on - - de fra

So - lae - - ra li on -

[70]

me di - ce - a, "Ec - - cho la piog - gia,

de fra me di - ce - a, "Ec -

[75]

Ec - cho Di - do et E - -

cho la piog - gia, Ec - cho Di - do

[80]

ne - - - - - - a."

et E - ne - - - - - - a."

With many hounds and with many falcons
We were hunting along the bank of the Adda,
And one shouted, "Hurry up!"
And another (called the dogs) "Vaccià, Varin, Torna, Picciola".
And another was catching the quails in flight.
When suddenly a storm broke and rain pelted down.

No greyhound ever raced through the countryside,
As (fast) as each of us did to escape the rain:
And one said, "Hey!
Give me my coat!" And then he said, "Give me my hat!"
I found shelter with my falcon
(In a place) where a shepherdess pierced my heart.

*Ritornello:*
She was alone there, and I said to myself,
"There is the rain; here are Dido and Aeneas."

# CHE PENA É QUEST' AL COR

BALLATA

FRANCESCO LANDINO

* Version for Keyboard instrument (probably not by Landino himself) as it appears in *Codex Faenza*.

82  *Francesco Landino*

*1* What pain it is to my heart that I cannot
*5* Use good manners
With these evil people,
(I hope) that I myself shall not be afflicted with envy.

*2* But really they will never deter me
from my determination, these envious ones.

*3* They probably will speak ill, if they speak at all
So that I won't follow my inclinations.

*4* For a long time now they have complained
*X* Not (indeed) with rudeness
But in such a manner
That they shall not make me turn red (with anger).

# LA QUARTE ESTAMPIE ROYALE

ANON

# SALTARELLO

*ANONYMOUS*

88

# AVE MARIS STELLA

HYMN

*JOHN DUNSTABLE*

1 Hail, star of the sea,
  Bountiful mother of God
  and ever Virgin,
  Blessed gate of heaven.

2 While Gabriel's voice
  Takes up that Hail,
  Secure us in peace
  Eva's name reversed.

3 Break the fetters of the accused;
  Bring forth light on blindness;
  Drive away our ills
  Request all goodness.

4 Show yourself to be mother
  May He receive our prayers through you
  He who has born for us
  And thought fit to be yours.

5 Virgin of all virgins
  mildest of all
  Free us from our sins
  Make us gentle and pure.

6 Help make our lives pure
  On our way to a safe place
  When we see Jesus
  We rejoice forever.

90  John Dunstable

# AVE MARIS STELLA

FAUXBOURDON HYMN

GUILLAUME DUFAY

A translation of this text appears on page 90.

# SE LA FACE AY PALE

CHANSON

GUILLAUME DUFAY

If my face looks pale
The chief fault lies with love
Indeed so much pain does it give me that I could drown myself in the sea
As the fair one that I serve well knows
I can neither know any joy nor live without her.

Se ay pesante malle
De dueil a porter,
Ceste amour est male
Pour moy de porter;
Car soy deporter
Ne veult devouloir,
Fors qu'a son vouloir
Obeisse, et puis
Qu'elle a tel pooir,
  Sans elle ne puis

If the burden of grief I bear is a heavy one
It is because this love is hard for me to bear
For she shows no wish to want to stop being harsh towards anyone who does no
   obey her every whim,
And such is her power over me that I cannot live without her.

C'est la plus reale
Qu'on puist regarder,
De s'amour leiale
Ne me puis guarder,
Fol sui de agarder
Ne faire devoir
D'amours recevoir
Fors d'elle, je cuij;
Se ne veil douloir,
  Sans elle ne puis.

She is the finest lady one could ever see.
I cannot help loving her faithfully, though I know I am a fool
To wait on her and not to seek love elsewhere.
While I have no wish to suffer, I cannot live without her.

# MISSA SE LA FACE AY PALE

KYRIE

GUILLAUME DUFAY

Canon: Tenor crescit in duplo

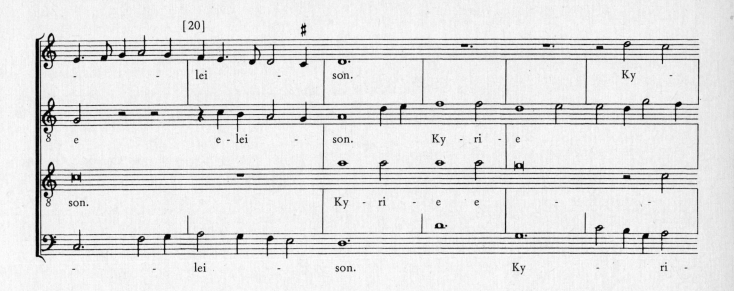

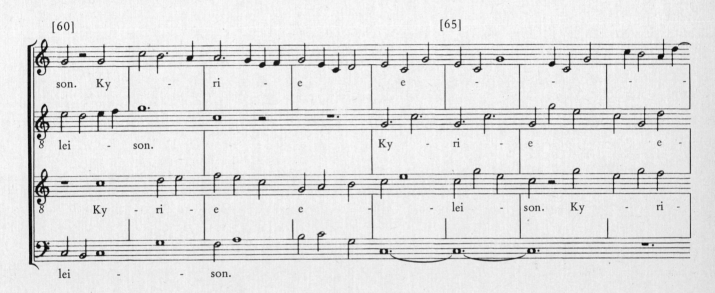

A translation of this text appears on page 4.

# CE JOUR DE L'AN VOUDRAY JOYE MENER

RONDEAU

GUILLAUME DUFAY

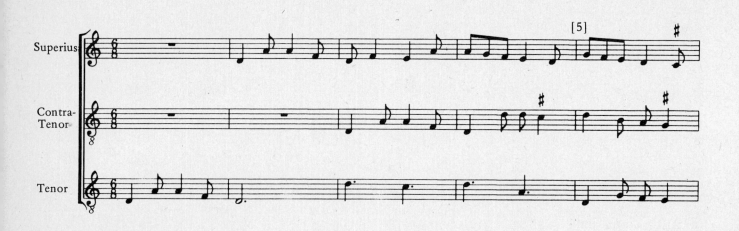

1,4,7   This New Year's day I will be joyful,
   Sing, dance and be of good cheer

 3 And certainly I will have enough power
   To be able to choose a new sweetheart

 5 To whom I can present
   My heart, person and wealth undivided:

2,8 To maintain the agreeable custom
   That all lovers are obliged to keep.

 6 Come god of love, be on my side
   So that fortune cannot grieve me.

2 Thou art empëress of heaven free;
 Now art thou mother in majesty,
 Y-knit in the blessëd Trinity;
  Regina celi, letare.

3 Hail wife, hail maidë, bright of ble!
 Hail daughter, hail sister full of pity!
 Hail cousin to the Persons Three!
  Regina celi, letare.

4 Lo, this courteous King of degree
 Will be thy Son with solempnity;
 Mild Mary, this is thy fee;
  Regina celi, letare.

5 Therefore kneel we on our knee;
 Thy blissful birth now worship we
 With this song of melody:
  Regina celi, letare.

100 *Guillaume Dufay*

# SING WE TO THIS MERRY COMPANY

FIFTEENTH CENTURY ENGLISH CAROL

# MISSA PROLATIONUM

AGNUS DEI

A translation of this text appears on page 13.

# MA MAÎTRESSE

RONDEAU

JEAN DE OCKEGHEM

1.5. Ma mai - stres - se et ma plus grant a - my -
4. In ces - sa - ment mon do-lent cuer l'ar - my -

- e, De mon de - sir la mor - tel - le en-ne -
- e, Dou - btant qu'en vous pi - tié soit en-dor

my - e, Par - fai - te en biens s'on - ques maiz le fut fem -
my - e, Qui ja ne soit, ma tant a - me - e da -

109

[20]

me, Cel-le seul — le de qui court
me, Maiz s'ain-sy est, si mal — heu —

[25]

bruit et fa — me. D'e stre sans per,
reux me cla — me Que plus ne quiers

[30]

ne vous ve-ray je my — — — e?
vi - vre heu — re ne de - my — — — e.

110  *Jean de Ockeghem*

[35]

2. He - las de vous     bien plain   - dre me de   -   vroi - e, S'il
3. Car sans vous voir     en quel   - que part que     soy   - e, Jout

[40]                                                          [45]

ne vous   plaist   que brief - ment vous   re - voy   - e, M'a -   mour,   par
ce que   voys   me des - plaist et   en - noy   - e, Ne   jus - qu'a

[50]

qui     d'aul - tre ay - mer     n'ay   puis - san   -   -   ce.
lors   je   n'au - ray   suf - fi - san   -   -   ce.

1  My mistress and my greatest friend,
   The mortal enemy of my desire,
   Perfect in qualities if ever woman was;
   She whom, alone, fame and rumor report
   As being without peer, shall I never see you?

2  Alas, I should indeed complain of you,
   If it does not please you to let me see you again shortly,
   My love, who make me unable to love another.

3  For without seeing you wherever I am,
   Everything that I see displeases and angers me,
   Nor shall I be satisfied until then.

4  Endlessly my sorrowing heart weeps,
   Fearing lest your pity have fallen asleep.
   May this never be my well-beloved lady,
   But if it is true, I am so unhappy
   That I do not wish to love an hour longer, nor even a half.

5  My mistress and my greatest friend,
   The mortal enemy of my desire,
   Perfect in qualities if ever woman was;
   She whom, alone, fame and rumor report
   As being without peer, shall I never see you?

# DE PLUS EN PLUS

RONDEAU

GILLES BINCHOIS

De plus en plus se re - nou - vel - le, Ma

[5] doul - ce da - me gen - te et bel - - - le,

[10] Ma vo - lon - té de vous - ve - ir.

[15] Ce me fait le tres grant de - sir Que j'ai de vous - ou -

[20] ir nou - vel - - - - - - - - le.

De plus en plus se renouvelle,
Ma doulce dame gente et belle,
Ma volonté de vous veir.

Ce me fait le tres grant desir
Que j'ai de vous ouir nouvelle.

Ne cuidiés pas que je recelle,
Comme a tous jours vous estes celle
Que je vueil de tout obeir.

De plus en plus …

Helas, se vous m'estes cruelle,
J'auroie au cuer angoisse telle
Que je voudroie bien morir,

Mais ce seroit sans desservir,
En soustenant vostre querelle.

De plus en plus …

Ce me fait le tres grant desir
Que j'ai de vous ouir nouvelle.

More and more there is renewed,
My sweet lady, noble and fair,
My will to see you.

Hence comes my very great desire
To hear news of you.

Do not think that I hold back,
Since always you are the one
Whom I wish to obey.

More and more there is renewed, …

Alas, if you are cruel to me
I shall have such anguish in my heart
That I shall want to die.

But this would be without abandoning your service
And still upholding your cause.

More and more there is renewed, …

Hence comes my very great desire
To hear news of you.

# BEATA ES, MARIA

MOTET

JACOB OBRECHT

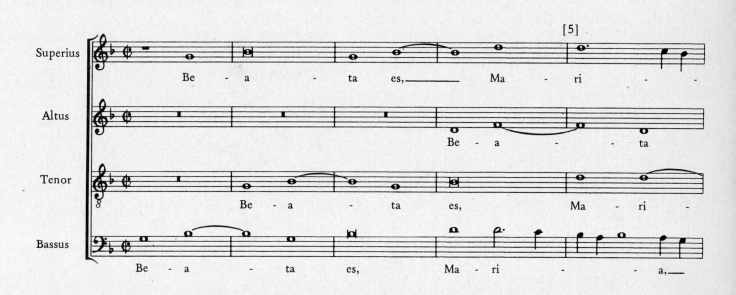

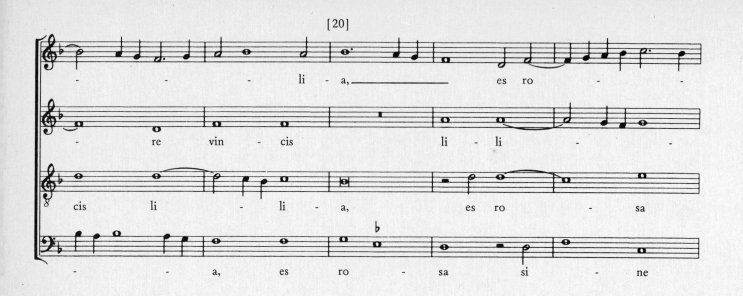

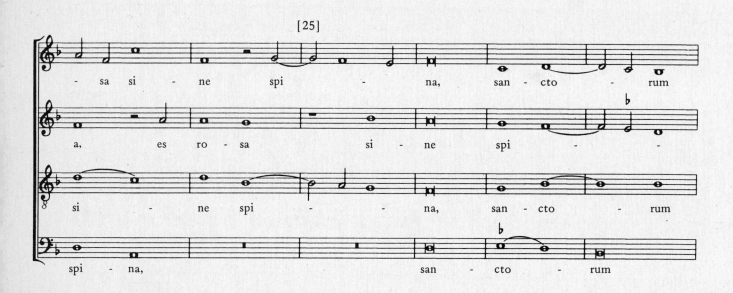

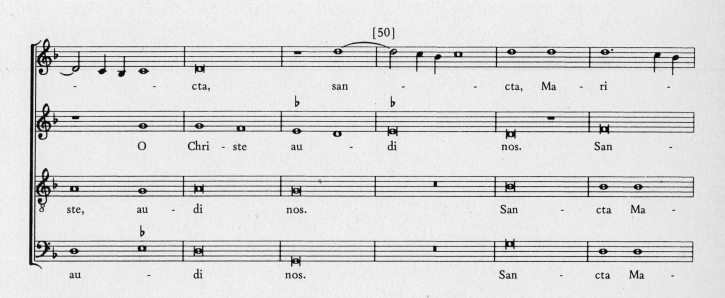

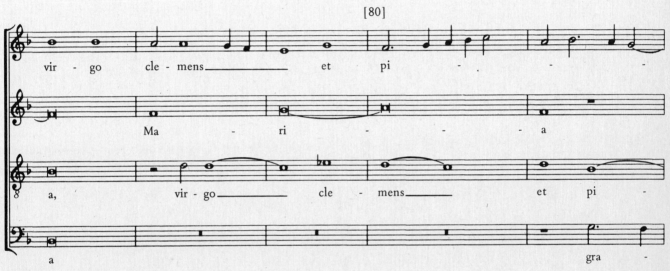

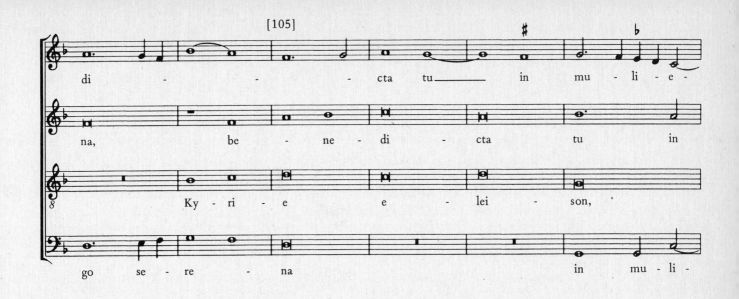

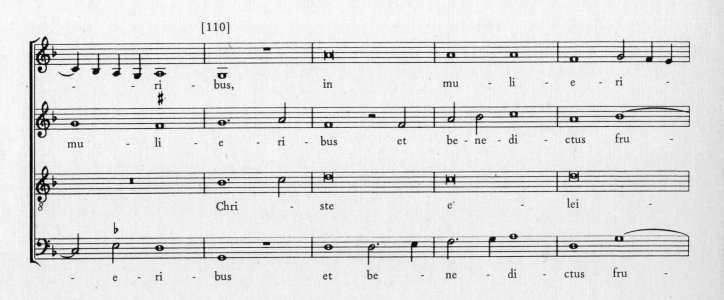

Beata es, Maria, virgo clemens et pia;
candore vincis lilia, es rosa sine spina,
sanctorum melodia.
Kyrie eleison, Christe eleison.
O Christe, audi nos.
Sancta, sancta, Maria, ora pro nobis
   ad Dominum.
O Christe, audi nos.

Ave Maria, virgo clemens et pia;
Gratia plena: Dominus tecum.
Virgo serena benedicta tu in mulieribus,
et benedictus fructus ventris tui, Jesus.
Ora pro nobis, Maria
ora pro nobis peccatoribus.
O Christe, audi nos.

You are blessed, Mary, gentle and holy virgin;
Whiter than a lily, a rose without thorns,
a holy melody.
Lord have mercy, Christ have mercy.
O Christ, hear us.
Holy, holy, Mary, pray for us to the Lord.

O Christ, hear us.

Hail Mary, gentle and holy virgin;
Full of grace: the Lord is with you.
Serene virgin you are blessed among women,
and blessed is the fruit of your womb, Jesus.
Pray for us, Mary
pray for us sinners.
O Christ, hear us.

# MISSA AVE MARIS STELLA

KYRIE

JOSQUIN DESPRÉS

124

A translation of this text appears on page 4.

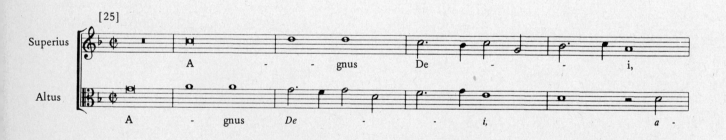

A translation of this text appears on page 13.

# ABSOLON, FILI MI

MOTET

JOSQUIN DESPRÉS

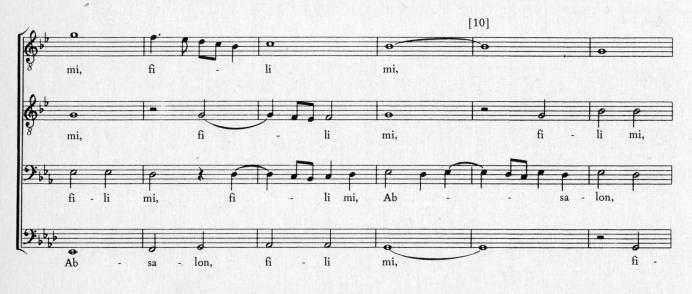

Absalom, my son, what would I not give to die for thee, my son Absalom?
May I live no longer, but descend into hell weeping.

# LA DÉPLORATION DE JOHAN OKEGHEM

MOTET-CHANSON

JOSQUIN DESPRÉS

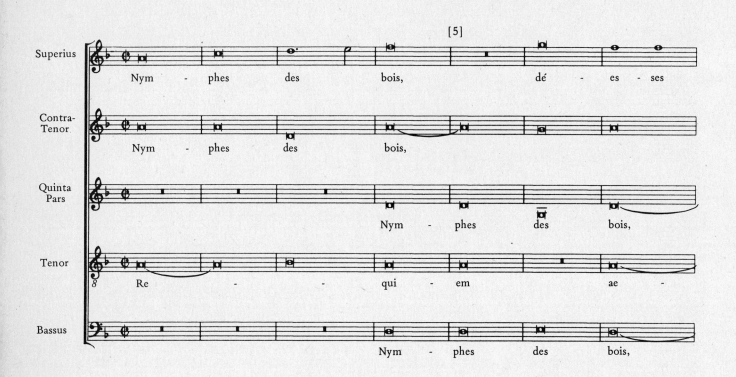

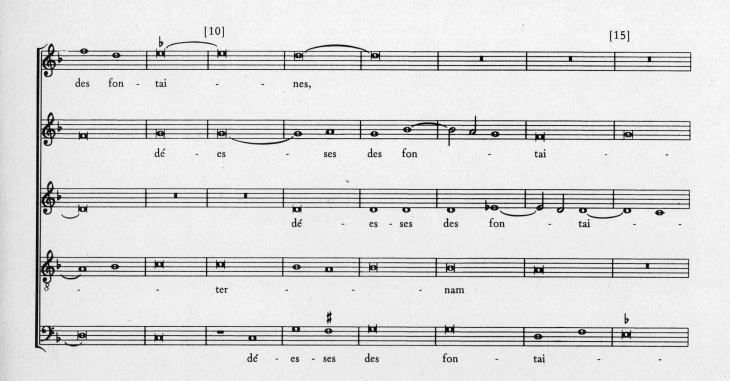

136

Nymphes des bois, déesses des fontaines,

Chantres expers de toutes nations,
Changez voz voix fort clères et haultaines
En cris tranchantz et lamentations.
Car d'Atropos les molestations
Vostr' Okeghem par sa rigeur attrape,
Le vray trésoir de musicque et chief d'oeuvre,
Qui de trépas désormais plus n'eschappe,
Dont grant doumaige est que la terre coeuvre.

*Cantus firmus:*
    Requiem aeternam dona eis Domine,
    et lux perpetua luceat eis.

Acoutrez vous d'abitz de deuil:
Josquin, Brumel, Pierchon, Compère.
Et plorez grosses larmes d'oeil:
Perdu avez vostre bon père.
Requiescat in pace. Amen.

Nymphs of the woods, goddesses
    of the streams,
Fine singers of every nation,
Change your bright and lofty voices
To piercing wails and lamentations.
For Atropos with cruel shears
Your Ockeghem has taken,
Music's very treasure and true master
From death can now no more escape,
And, grievous loss, in earth lies buried.

Eternal rest grant them, O Lord,
Let your everlasting light shine on them.

Clothe yourselves in deepest mourning,
Josquin, Brumel, Pierchon, Compère.
And from your eyes shed flooding tears:
For you have lost your good father.
May he rest in peace. Amen.

# FAULTE D'ARGENT

CHANSON

JOSQUIN DESPRÉS

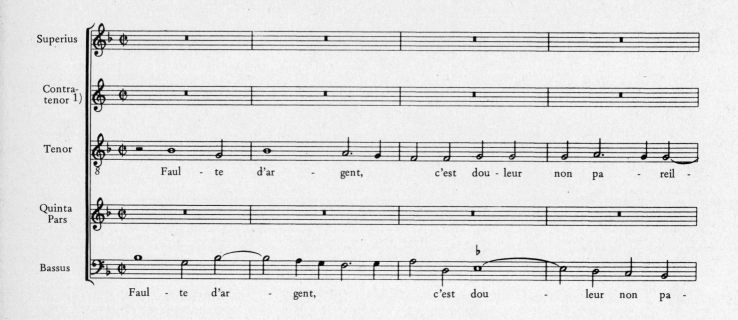

1) Canon: Faulte d'argent par Nature,
   Faulte d'argent par B mollis.

Faulte d'argent, c'est douleur non pareille
Se je le dis, las, je sais bien pourquoy:
Sans de quibus, il fault se tenir quoy.

Femme qui dort, pour argent se resveille.

Lack of money is painful beyond measure,
And if I say so, alas, I know well why:
An empty pocket means that one must
  keep quiet.

But a sleeping woman awakes for gold.

# EIN' FESTE BURG IST UNSER GOTT

Ein fe-ste Burg ist un-ser Gott, ein gu-te Wehr und Waf - fen;
er hilft uns frei aus al - ler Not, die uns jetzt hat be-trof - fen;

Der al - te bö - se Feind mit Ernst ers jetzt meint; gross Macht und viel

List sein grau-sam Rü-stung ist; auf Erd ist nicht seins Glei - - chen.

1 A stronghold sure is our God,
  A trusty shield and sword;
  He sets us free from every need,
  That ever beset us.
  The ancient evil foe
  Now thinks earnestly,
  With great might and wily craft, he makes his cruel preparations,
  On earth he has no equal.

a)

*JOHANN WALTER*

Cantus

Ein fe - ste Burg ist un - - - ser
Er hilft uns frei aus al - - - ler

Tenor

Ein fe - ste Burg ist un - ser
Er hilft uns frei aus al - ler

[5]

Gott,_____ ein gu-te_____ Wehr und Waf - - fen.
Not,_____ die uns jetzt_____ hat be-trof - - fen.

Gott,_____ ein gu-te Wehr und Waf - - fen.
Not,_____ die uns jetzt hat be-trof - - fen.

[10]                                      [15]

Der al - te bö - se Feind mit Ernst ers jetzt meint;

Der alt_____ bö - se Feind mit Ernst ers jetzt meint;

gross Macht und viel List sein grau-sam Rü - stung ist;

gross Macht und viel List sein grau - sam Rü - stung ist;

auf Erd ist nicht seins glei - - chen.

auf Erd ist nicht seins glei - - chen.

# EIN' FESTE BURG IST UNSER GOTT

JOHANN WALTER

151

152  *Johann Walter*

# EIN' FESTE BURG

AD AEQUALES

JOHANN WALTER

c)

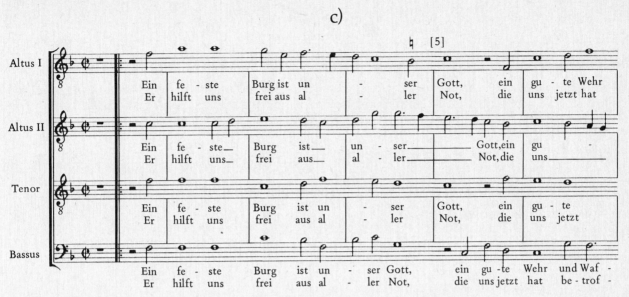

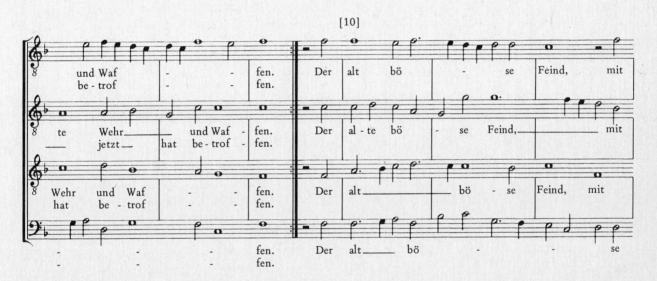

[20]

sam Rü - stung ist; auf Erd ist ____ nicht seins Glei - - - chen.

Rü - stung ist; auf Erd ist nicht ____ seins Glei - chen.

sam Rü - stung ist; auf Erd ist nicht seins Glei - chen.

Rü - stung ist; ____ auf ____ Erd ist nicht seins Glei - - chen.

154  *Johann Walter*

# IO NON COMPRO PIÚ SPERANZA

FROTTOLA

MARCO CARA

Io non com - pro più spe - ran - za Ché gliè fal - sa mer - can - ci - a. A dar sol at - ten - do vi - a Quel - la po - ca che m'a - van - za. Io non com - pro più spe - ran - za Ché gliè fal - sa mer - can - ci - a, ché gliè fal - sa mer - can - ci - a.

155

| | |
|---|---|
| Io non compro più speranza | I no longer buy hope |
| Ché gli è falsa mercancia, | Because it is counterfeit merchandise, |
| A dar sol attendo via | I am just waiting to give away |
| Quella poca che m'avanza. | The little that I have left. |
| Io non compro più speranza | I no longer buy hope |
| Ché gli è falsa mercancia. | Because it is counterfeit merchandise. |
| | |
| Cara un tempo la comprai, | Once I bought it at a high price, |
| Hor la vendo a bon mercato | Now I sell it very cheap |
| E consiglio ben che mai | And I advise that never |
| Non ne compri un sventurato | Should a misfortunate one buy it. |
| Ma più presto nel suo stato | But rather in his condition as it is |
| Se ne resti con costanza. | He should remain contented. |
| Io non ... | I no longer ... |
| | |
| El sperare è come el sogno | Hoping is like dreaming |
| Che per più riesce in nulla, | That usually results in nothing, |
| El sperar è proprio il bisogno | Hoping is truly the need |
| De chi al vento si trastulla, | Of him who plays in the wind, |
| El sperare sovente a nulla, | Hoping often brings nothing |
| Chi continua la sua danza. | To him who continues to dance. |
| Io non ... | I no longer ... |

156   *Marco Cara*

# IL BIANCO E DOLCE CIGNO

MADRIGAL

JACOB ARCADELT

Il bian - co e dol - ce ci - gno can - tan - do mo - re. Et

Il bian - co e dol - ce ci - gno can - tan - do mo - re. Et

Il bian - co e dol - ce ci - gno can - tan - do mo - re. Et

Et

io pian - gen - do giung' al fin del vi - ver mi - o, et

io pian - gen - do giung' al fin del vi - ver mi - o, et

io pian - gen - do giung' al fin del vi - ver mi - o, et

io pian - gen - do giung' al fin del vi - ver mi - o, et

io pian - gen - do giung' al fin del vi - ver mi - o, stran'

io pian - gen - do giung' al fin del vi - ver mi - o, stran'

io pian - gen - do giung' al fin del vi - ver mi - o, stran'

io pian - gen - do giung' al fin del vi - ver mi - o,

158  *Jacob Arcadelt*

The white and gentle swan sings when dying
And I, crying, approach the end of my life.
How strange the difference,
that he dies disconsolate
and I die happy.
For death fills me with joy and desire.
Since at death I feel no other pain,
I would be content to die a thousand times.

160  *Jacob Arcadelt*

# PETITE NYMPHE FOLASTRE

CHANSON

CLÉMENT JANEQUIN

164 Clément Janequin

Playful little nymph
Little nymph that I adore
My darling, in whose eyes
Live my worst and my best.

My demure one, my sweet
My gracious one, my idol
To satisfy me, you must agree
A thousand times a day to kiss.

# FANTASIA NO. 8

FOR VIHUELA

*LUIS DE MILÁN*

FANTASIA NO. 8  167

# RICERCARE QUARTO

FOR ORGAN

GEROLAMO CAVAZZONI

[5]

[10]

[15]

[20]

# DIFERENCIAS SOBRE EL "CANTO DEL CAVALLERO"

ANTONIO DE CABEZÓN

173

174  Antonio de Cabezón

# TWO DANCES

RONDO

*TILMAN SUSATO*

Saltarello

# O MAGNUM MYSTERIUM

MOTET

ADRIAN WILLAERT

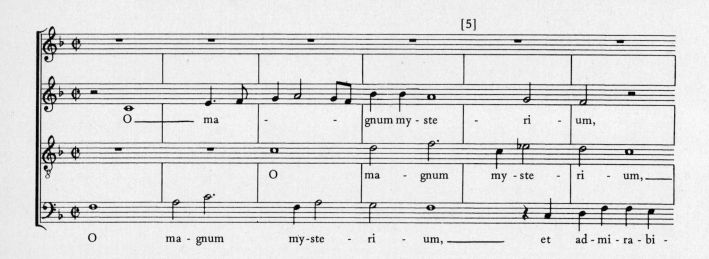

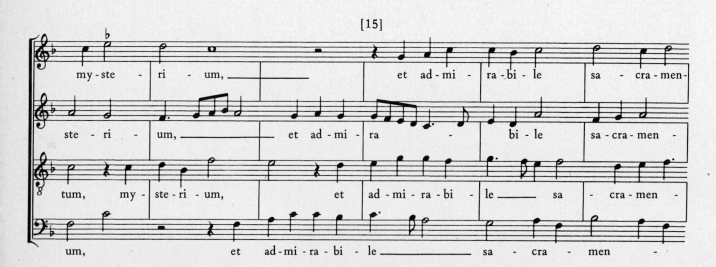

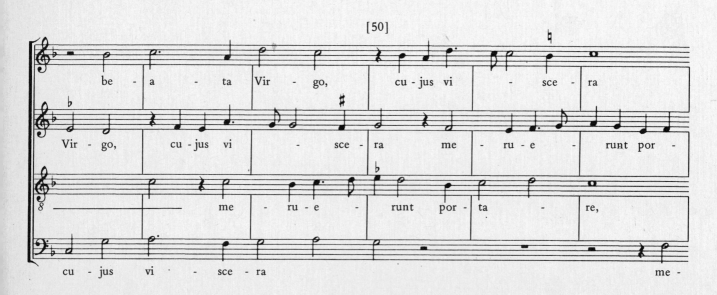

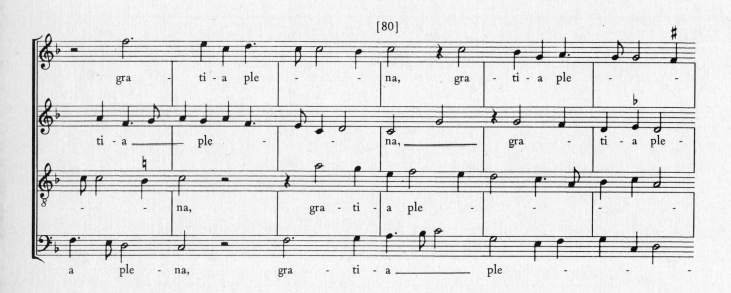

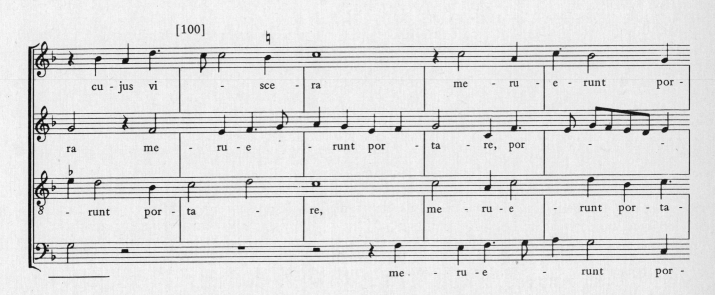

O great mystery and admirable sacrament
that the animals should witness the birth of the Lord, lowly, in a stable.
Blessed Virgin, whose womb is worthy of carrying the Lord, Jesus Christ.

Hail Mary, full of grace, the Lord is with you,
Blessed Virgin, whose womb is worthy of carrying the Lord, Jesus Christ.

# O MAGNUM MYSTERIUM

MOTET

GIOVANNI PIERLUIGI DA PALESTRINA

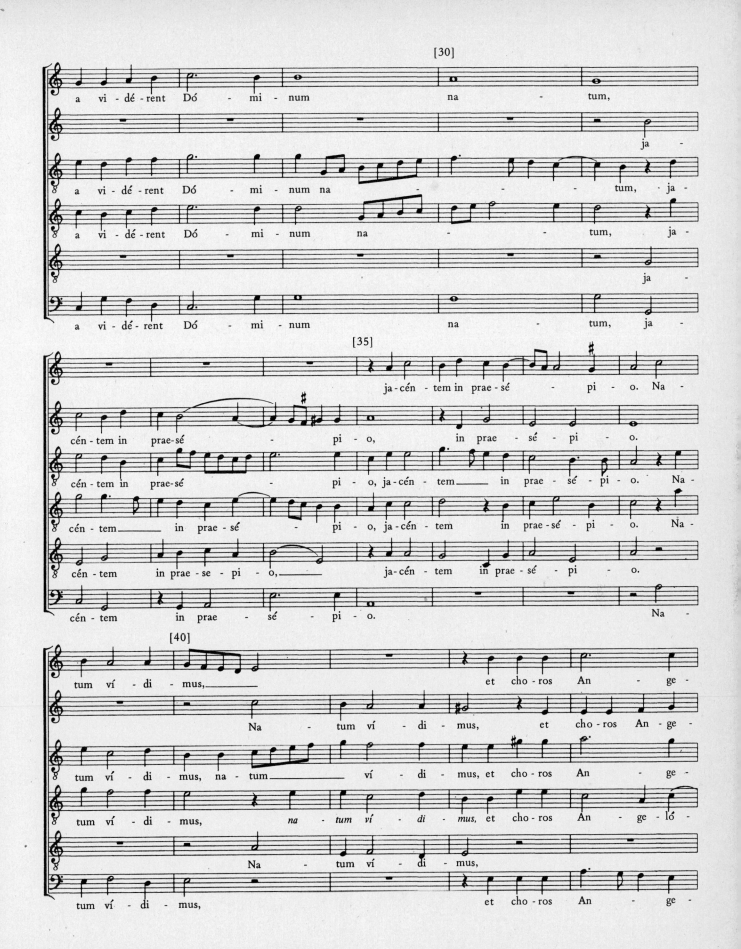

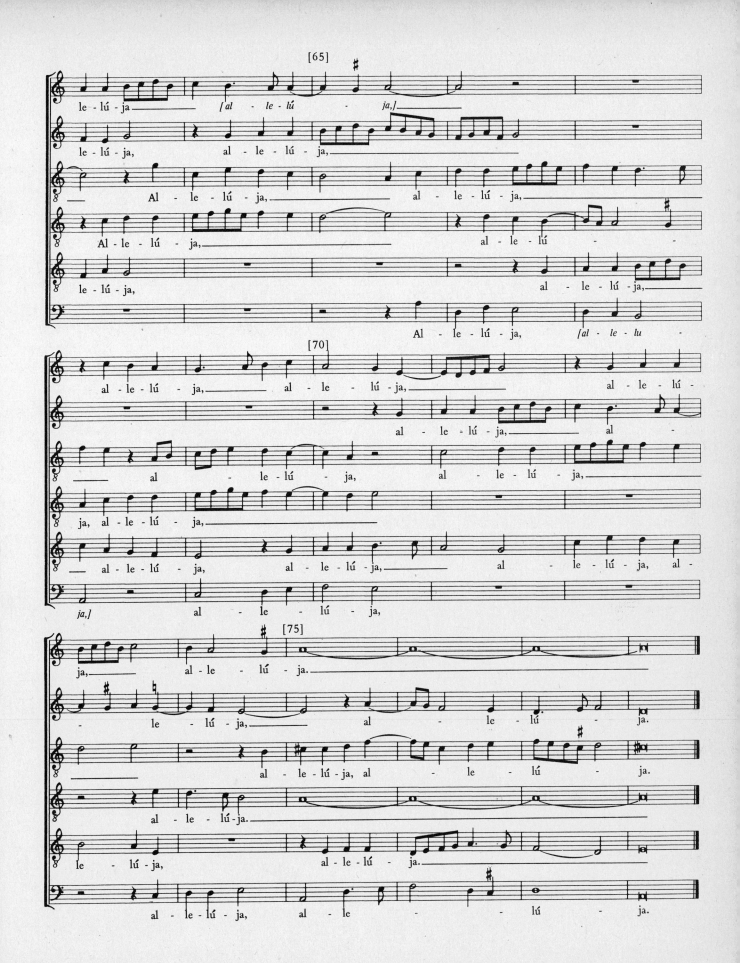

SECUNDA PARS.

190 *Giovanni Pierluigi da Palestrina*

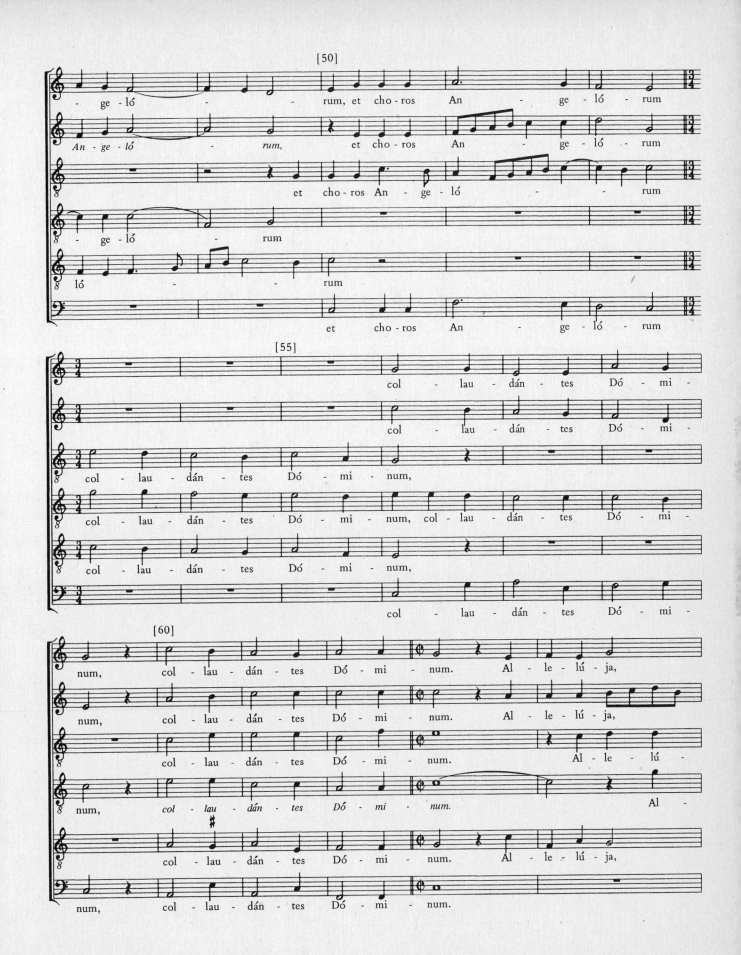

O great mystery and admirable sacrament
that the animals should witness the birth of the Lord, lowly, in a stable.
We see him born and choirs of angels praising the Lord, Alleluia.

What did you see, shepherds? Tell us:
speak out, who has appeared?
We saw him born . . .

# MISSA O MAGNUM MYSTERIUM

KYRIE

GIOVANNI PIERLUIGI DA PALESTRINA

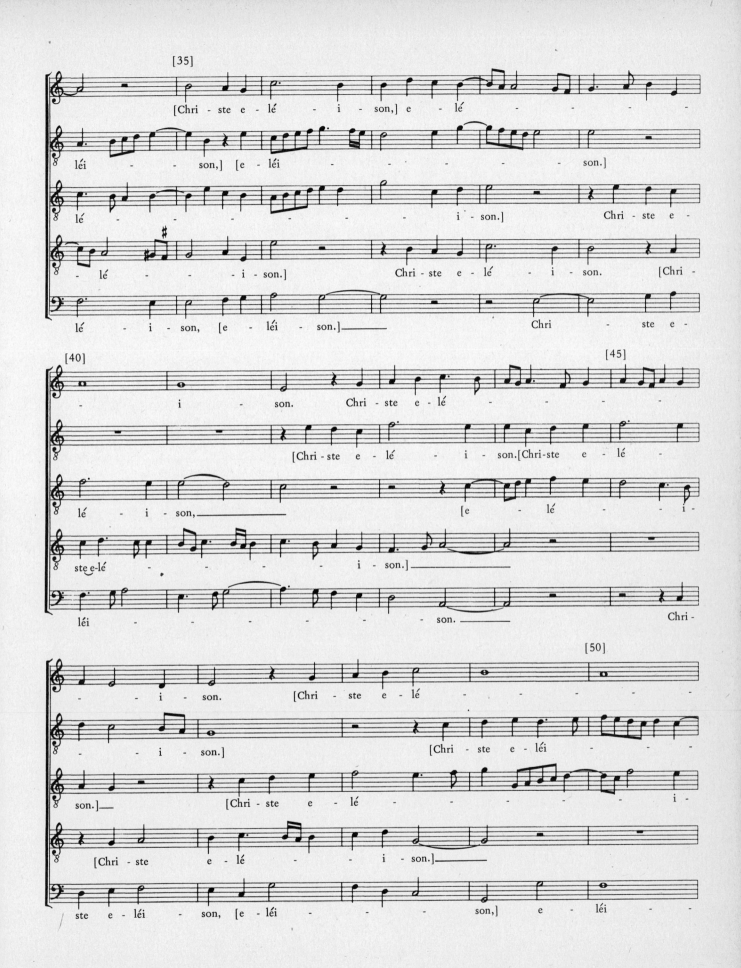

A translation of this text appears on page 4.

*Giovanni Pierluigi da Palestrina*

The sections  of this movement set to the text

Qui tollis peccata mundi miserere nobis, suscipe deprecationem nostram
Qui sedes ad dexteram Patris, miserere nobis
Quoniam tu solus sanctus, tu solus Dominus, tu solus Altissimus, Jesu Christe

have been omitted.

A translation of this text appears on page 6.

*Giovanni Pierluigi da Palestrina*

The sections of this movement set to the texts

   Crucifixus etiam pro nobis sub Pontio Pilato, passus, et sepultus est.

   Et resurrexit tertia die secundum Scriptums.

   Et ascendit in coelum, sedet ad dexteram Patris.
   Et iterum venturus est.
   Cum gloria judicare vivos et mortuos, cujus regni non erit finis.

   Et in Spiritum Sanctum, Dominum, et vivificantem qui ex Patri Filioque procedit
   Qui cum Patre et Filio simul adoratur, et conglorificatur, qui locutus est per Prophetas.

   Et unam sanctam catholicam et Apostolicam Ecclesiam.

have been omitted.

210  *Giovanni Pierluigi da Palestrina*

A translation of this text appears on page 8.

A translation of this text appears on page 12.

The sections of this movement set to the texts

    Pleni sunt coeli et terra gloria tua.

    Hosanna in excelsis.

    Benedictus qui venit in nomine Domini.

have been omitted.

## AGNUS DEI II

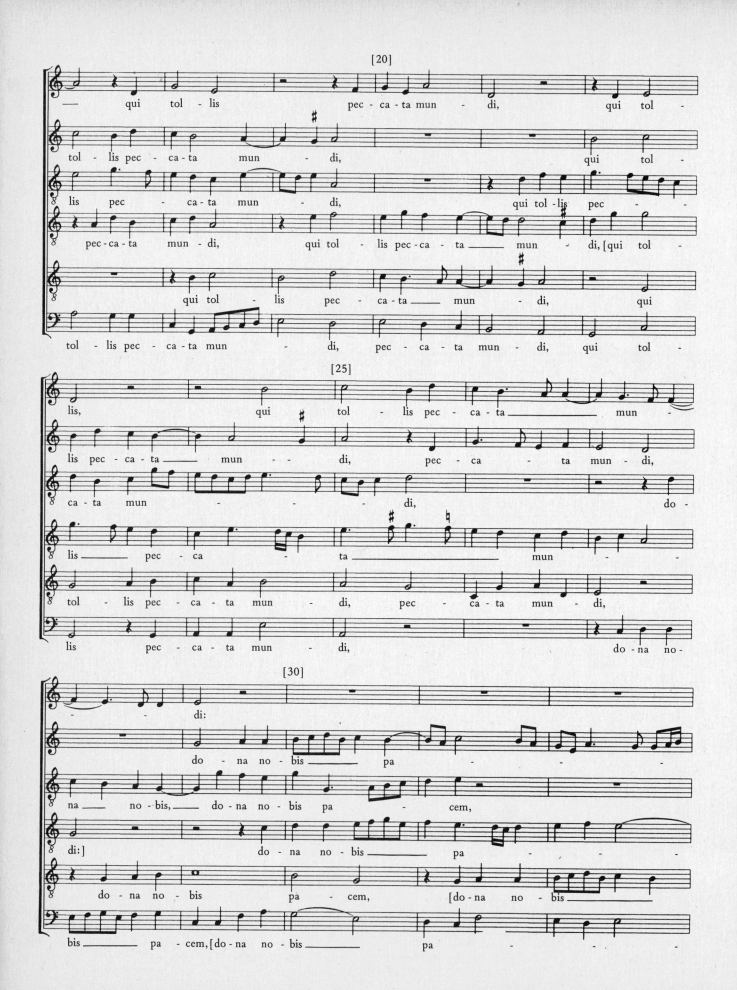

A translation of this text appears on page 13.

# O MAGNUM MYSTERIUM

MOTET

TOMÁS LUIS DE VICTORIA

A translation of this text appears on page 15.

# O MAGNUM MYSTERIUM

MOTET

WILLIAM BYRD

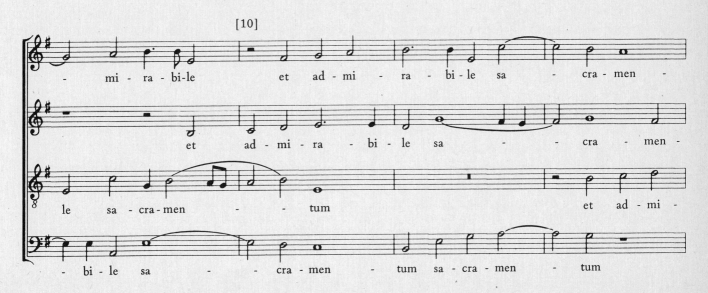

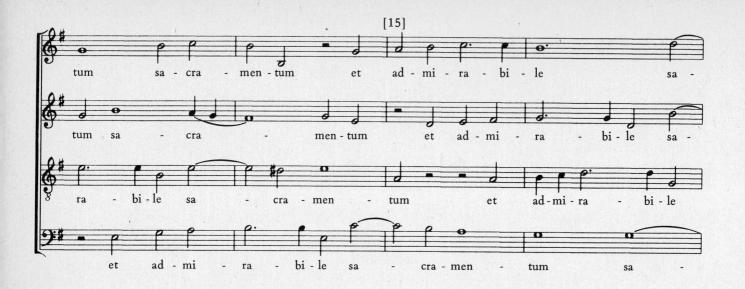

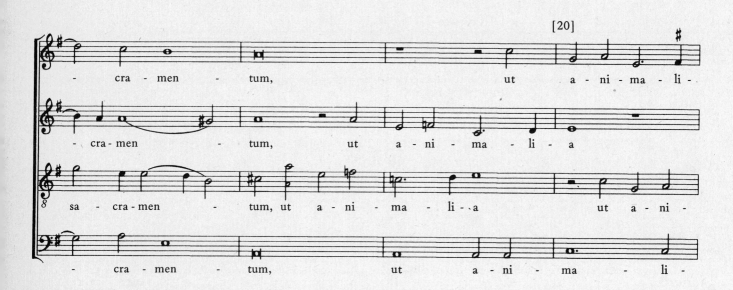

226   *William Byrd*

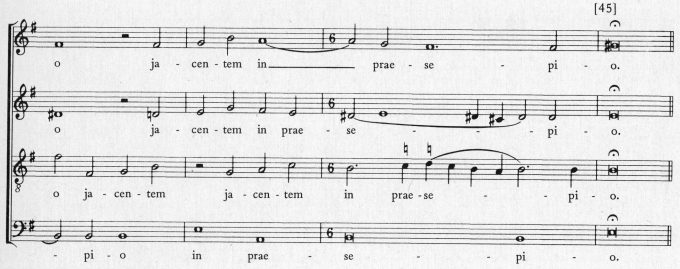

**SECUNDA PARS**

228 · *William Byrd*

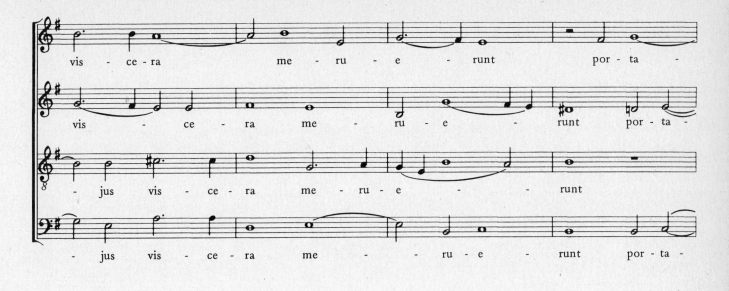

vis - ce - ra     me - ru - e - runt     por - ta -

vis - ce - ra     me - ru - e - runt     por - ta -

- jus vis - ce - ra     me - ru - e - runt

- jus vis - ce - ra     me - ru - e - runt     por - ta -

[55]

- re por - ta - re Do - mi - num Chris -

- re por - ta - re Do - mi - num Chris - tum Chris -

por - ta - re Do - mi - num Chris - tum Chris -

- re por - ta - re Do - mi - num Chris -

[60]

- tum Do - mi - num Chris - tum.     *Fine*

- tum Do - mi - num Chris - tum.     *Fine*

tum Do - mi - num Chris - tum.     *Fine*

tum Do - mi - num Chris - tum.     *Fine*

VERSUS

[65]

[70]

[75]

Repeat *Beata Virgo* down to *Christum*.
Then *ad lib.* the first part, *O magnum mysterium*.

A translation of this text appears on page 15.

230  *William Byrd*

# TRISTIS EST ANIMA MEA

MOTET

ORLANDO DI LASSO

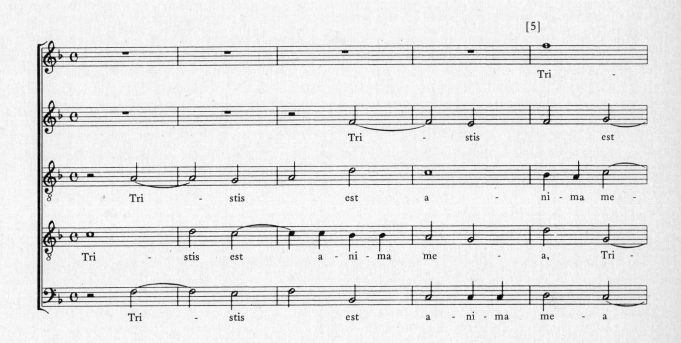

*TRISTIS EST ANIMA MEA 233*

My soul is sorrowful, even unto death;
wait here, and watch with me:
now you will see the multitude that will surround me;
you will run away, and I will go to be sacrificed for you.

# O MAGNUM MYSTERIUM

POLYCHORAL MOTET

GIOVANNI GABRIELI

238  *Giovanni Gabrieli*

A translation of this text appears on page 15.

# EIN' FESTE BURG IST UNSER GOTT

*MICHAEL PRAETORIUS*

a)

A translation of this text appears on page 149.

## b)

3 And if the world were full of devils,
  Ready to devour us,
  We need not be afraid,
  In spite of all we would succeed.
  The Prince of this world,
  However grim he would be, cannot avail,
  His authority will surely stand trial,
  The smallest word will bring his downfall.

246 *Michael Praetorius*

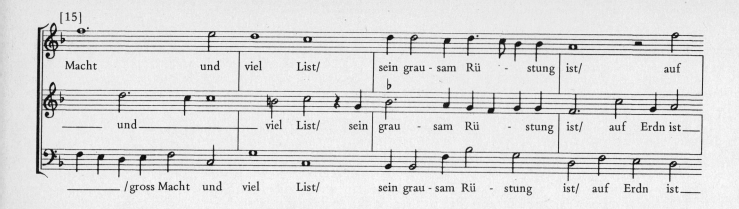

248  *Michael Praetorius*

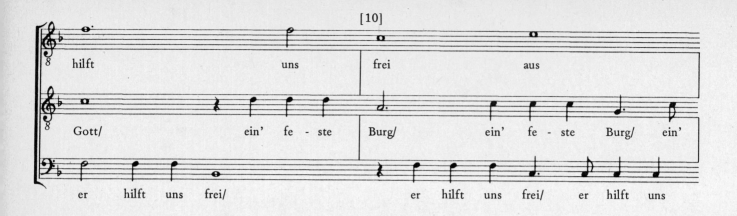

250  *Michael Praetorius*

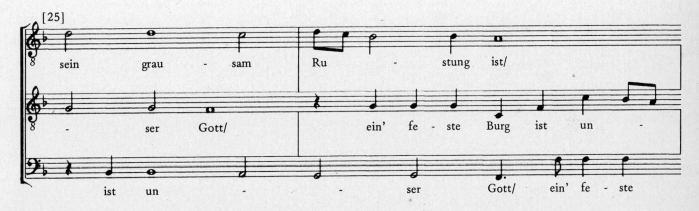

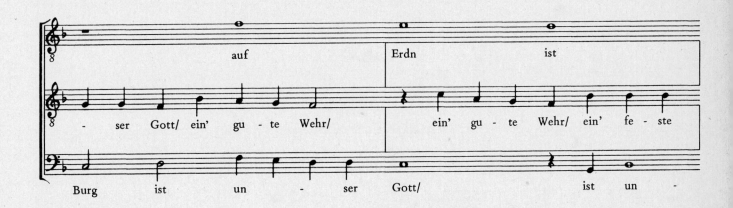

# THIS IS THE RECORD OF JOHN

VERSE ANTHEM

ORLANDO GIBBONS

This is the re-cord of John, when the Jews sent

priests and Le-vites from Je-ru-sa-lem, from Je-ru-sa-lem to ask

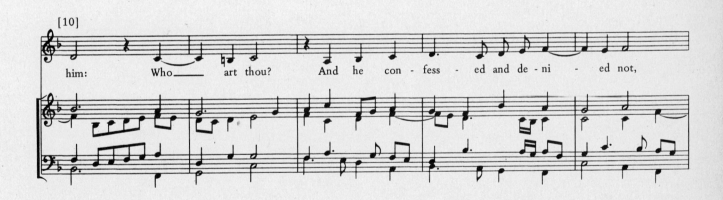

him: Who art thou? And he con-fess-ed and de-ni-ed not,

and said plain-ly: I am not the Christ.

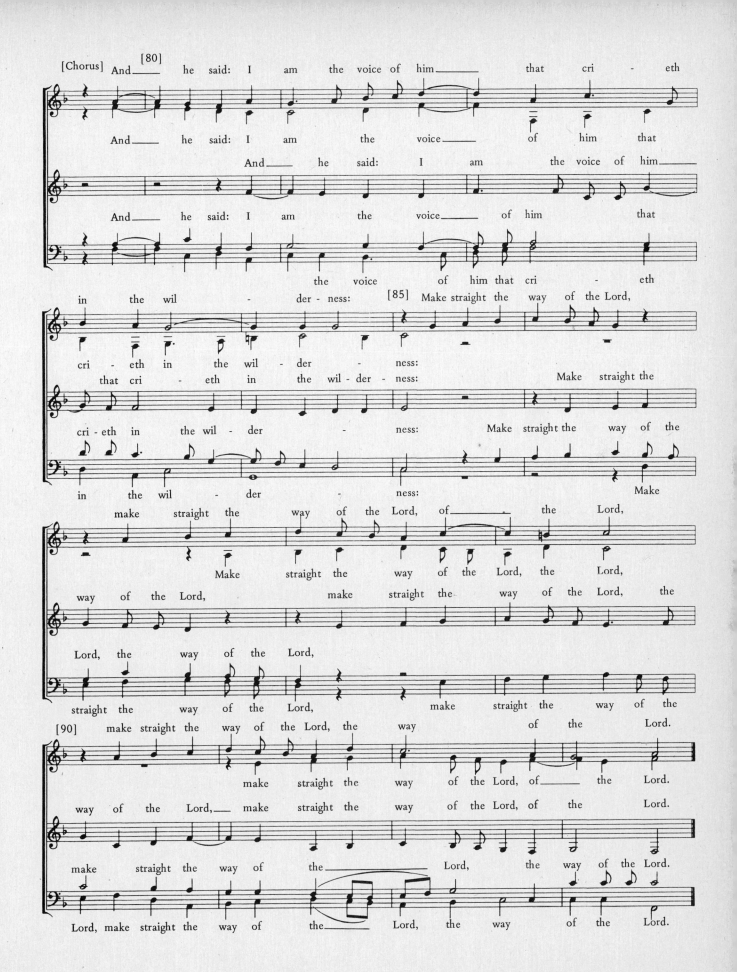

# BON JOUR MON COEUR

CHANSON

ORLANDO DI LASSO

Good day my heart! Good day my sweet life, Good day my eye, Good day my sweetheart. Ah! good day my pretty one, My sweet one, Good day my delight, my love, My sweet spring time, My sweet new flower, My sweet pleasure, My sweet dove, My lark, My fair turtledove! Good day my sweet rebel.

# AMOR VITTORIOSO

BALLETTO

GIOVANNI GASTOLDI

Canto: Tut - ti ve - ni - te ar - ma - ti, O for - ti miei sol - da - ti,

Quinto: Tut - ti ve - ni - te ar - ma - ti, O for - ti miei sol - da - ti,

Alto: Tut - ti ve - ni - te ar - ma - ti, O for - ti miei sol - da - ti,

Tenore: Tut - ti ve - ni - te ar - ma - ti, O for - ti miei sol - da - ti,

Basso: Tut - ti ve - ni - te ar - ma - ti, O for - ti miei sol - da - ti,

[5]

fa la la la la la la, fa la la la la la,

fa la la la la la la la la la, fa la la la la,

fa la la la la la la la, fa la la la la la la la,

fa la la la la la la, fa la la, fa la la la la la la la la,

fa la la la la la la, fa la la la la la la,

[10]

Tut - ti ve - ni - te ar - ma - ti, O for - ti miei sol - da - ti,

Tut - ti ve - ni - te ar - ma - ti, O for - ti miei sol - da - ti,

Tut - ti ve - ni - te ar - ma - ti, O for - ti miei sol - da - ti,

Tut - ti ve - ni - te ar - ma - ti, O for - ti miei sol - da - ti,

Tut - ti ve - ni - te ar - ma - ti, O for - ti miei sol - da - ti,

262 *Giovanni Gastoldi*

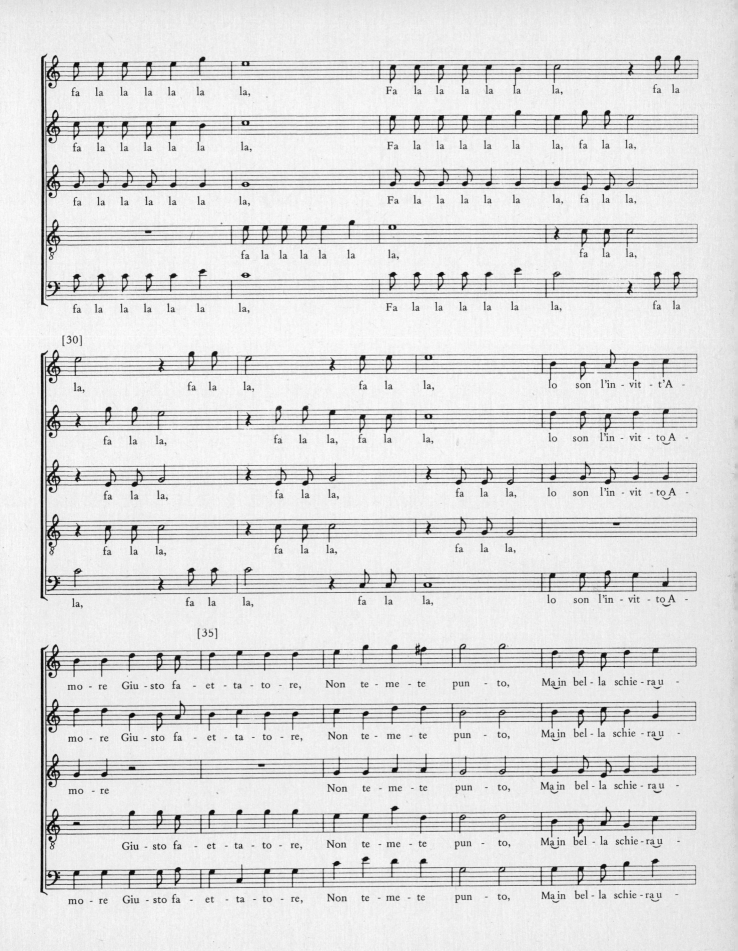

**[40]**

ni - ti, Me se-gui-ta-te ar - di - ti, fa la la la la la la,

ni - ti, Me se-gui-ta-te ar - di - ti, fa la la la la la la,

ni - ti, Me se-gui-ta-te ar - di - ti, fa la la la la la la,

ni - ti, Me se-gui-ta-te ar - di - ti, Fa la la la la la

ni - ti, Me se-gui-ta-te ar - di - ti, fa la la la la la la,

**[45]**

Fa la la la la la la, fa la la, fa la la, fa la la.

Fa la la la la la la, fa la la, fa la la, fa la la, fa la la.

Fa la la la la la la, fa la la, fa la la, fa la la la la la.

la, fa la la, fa la la, fa la la la la la.

Fa la la la la la la, fa la la, fa la la, fa la la.

1 Tutti venite armati  
  O forti miei soldati, fa la la  
  Io son l'invitt' Amore  
  Giusto saettatore  
  Non temete punto  
  Ma in bella schiera uniti  
  Me seguitate arditi, fa la la

             Come with your weapons ready  
             my strong soldiers, fa la la  
             I am the unconquered love  
             Fair archer  
             Do not fear anything at all  
             But, united in well-ordered ranks,  
             Follow me, you bold ones, fa la la

2 Sembrano forti heroi  
  Quei che son contra voi, fa la la  
  Ma da chi sà ferire  
  Non si sapran schermite  
  Non temete punto  
  Ma corraggiosi e forti  
  Siat'a la pugna accorti, fa la la

             They appear to be strong heroes  
             Those who are against you, fa la la  
             But from whom did they learn how to fight  
             They do not know how to fence  
             Do not fear anything at all  
             But, courageous and strong,  
             Be on your guard in the battle, fa la la

3 Lieti hor movete il piede  
  Che vostre sian le prede, fa la la  
  Hor via feriam lo sdegno  
  Ch'ei de la vita è indegno  
  Non temete punto  
  Eterna fia la gloria  
  E certa è la vittoria, fa la la

             Happily now stir your feet  
             Because the spoils are yours, fa la la  
             Now we shall chase away your anger  
             Because those who are alive are unworthy  
             Do not fear anything at all  
             Glory will be eternal  
             And victory is certain, fa la la

4 Già morto giace in terra  
  Chi ci havea mosso guerra, fa la la  
  Hor gli altri suoi seguaci  
  Tutti affaliamo audaci  
  Non temete punto  
  Ecco ch'i non estinti  
  Fuggon già sparti e vinti, fa la la.

             Already dead and lying on the ground  
             Are those who have had too much war, fa la la  
             Now the rest of his followers  
             Feign daring  
             Do not fear anything at all  
             Because those who are not dead  
             Will flee divided and vanquished, fa la la.

# SOLO E PENSOSO

MADRIGAL

LUCA MARENZIO

266

Seconda Parte

272 *Luca Marenzio*

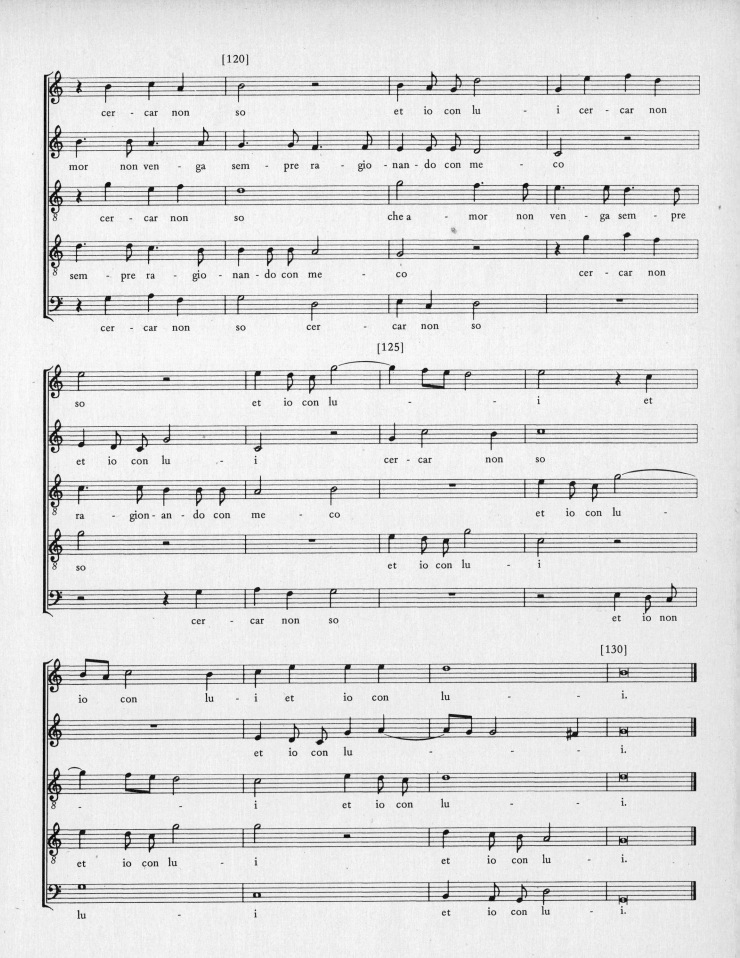

Alone and pensive, the most deserted fields
I pace with steps lagging and slow,
And I hold my eyes watchfully, in order to flee
Wherever human traces mark the sand.
No other screen do I find to protect me
From people's manifest awareness,
Because in my acts bereft of joy
They can read from without how inwardly I blaze:

So that I now believe mountains and shores
And rivers and forests know of what temper
My life is, hidden from others.
And yet pathways so rough or wild
I do not know how to seek, that love would not always come
Reasoning with me, and I with him.

276  *Luca Marenzio*

# REVECY VENIR DU PRINTEMPS

MUSIQUE MESURÈE

CLAUDE LEJEUNE

RECHANT À 5

CHANT À 2

Le ca-nard s'é-bat à plon - ger, Et fo-las-tre a-mour va cher-chant,

Ja la grue a fait a-lon-ger sa ba-tail-le à poin - te four - chant.

## RECHANT À 5

Re - voi - cy ve - nir du Prin - temps L'a - mou - reus le dous et beau temps.

Re - voi - cy ve - nir du Prin - temps L'a - mou - reus le dous et beau temps.

Re - voi - cy ve - nir du Prin - temps L'a - mou - reus le dous et beau temps.

Re - voi - cy ve - nir du Prin - temps L'a - mou - reus le dous et beau temps.

Re - voi - cy ve - nir du Prin - temps L'a - mou - reus le dous et beau temps.

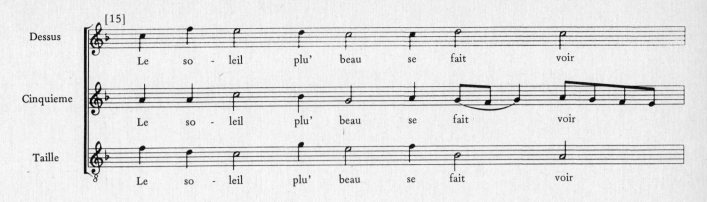

Le so - leil plu' beau se fait voir

Le so - leil plu' beau se fait voir

Le so - leil plu' beau se fait voir

Plu' se - rain, plu' clair, plu' ver - meil, Le nua - ge é - pais se voit choir

Plu' se - rain, plu' clair, plu' ver - meil, Le nua - ge é - pais se voit choir

Plu' se - rain, plu' clair, plu' ver - meil, Le nua - ge é - pais se voit choir

Dis - si - pé du ray du grand oeil Mi - le bois de verd se font pleins,

Dis - si - pé du ray du grand oeil Mi - le bois de verd se font pleins,

Dis - si - pé du ray du grand oeil Mi - le bois de verd se font pleins,

Mi - le champs de verd se sont peins, Mi - le prés De fleurs bi - gar - rés.

Mi - le champs de verd se sont peins, Mi - le prés De fleurs bi - gar - rés.

Mi - le champs de verd se sont peins, Mi - le prés De fleurs bi - gar - rés.

## RECHANT À 5

Re - voi - cy ve - nir du Prin - temps L'a - mou - reus le dous et beau temps.

Re - voi - cy ve - nir du Prin - temps L'a - mou - reus le dous et beau temps.

Re - voi - cy ve - nir du Prin - temps L'a - mou - reus le dous et beau temps.

Re - voi - cy ve - nir du Prin - temps L'a - mou - reus le dous et beau temps.

Re - voi - cy ve - nir du Prin - temps L'a - mou - reus le dous et beau temps.

## CHANT À 4

Dessus — Ja le fis mi - gnard de Ve - nus A sa loy ce tout se sou - met,

Haute-Contre — Ja le fis mi - gnard de Ve - nus A sa loy ce tout se sou - met,

Taille — Ja le fis mi - gnard de Ve - nus A sa loy ce tout se sou - met,

Basse-Contre — Ja le fis mi - gnard de Ve - nus A sa loy ce tout se sou - met,

Mi - le coeurs d'a - mour ja sont meus, Mi - le coeurs bles - sés de son trait,

Mi - le coeurs d'a - mour ja sont meus, Mi - le coeurs bles - sés de son trait,

Mi - le coeurs d'a - mour ja sont meus, Mi - le coeurs bles - sés de son trait,

Mi - le coeurs d'a - mour ja sont meus, Mi - le coeurs bles - sés de son trait,

280 *Claude Lejeune*

Jus - que dans le sein de The - tis Le pois - son d'a - mour se sent point,

Jus - que dans le sein de The - tis Le pois - son d'a - mour se sent point,

Jus - que dans le sein de The - tis Le pois - son d'a - mour se sent point,

Jus - que dans le sein de The - tis Le pois - son d'a - mour se sent point,

[30]

L'a - ni - mal de l'air y est pris, Su' la terre, hé! Quel ne l'est point?

L'a - ni - mal de l'air y est pris, Su' la terre, hé! Quel ne l'est point?

L'a - ni - mal de l'air y est pris, Su' la terre, hé! Quel ne l'est point?

L'a - ni - mal de l'air y est pris, Su' la terre, hé! Quel ne l'est point?

RECHANT, CHANT ET RECHANT Á 5

[32]

Re - voi - cy ve - nir du Prin - temps, L'a - mou - reus, le dous et beau temps.

Re - voi - cy ve - nir du Prin - temps, L'a - mou - reus, le dous et beau temps.

Re - voi - cy ve - nir du Prin - temps, L'a - mou - reus, le dous et beau temps.

Re - voi - cy ve - nir du Prin - temps, L'a - mou - reus, le dous et beau temps.

Re - voi - cy ve - nir du Prin - temps, L'a - mou - reus, le dous et beau temps.

I' nou' faut aus-si fré-quen - ter Les é - bas, l'a-mour et les jeus,

I' nou' faut aus-si fré-quen - ter Les é - bas, l'a-mour et les jeus,

I' nou' faut aus-si fré-quen - ter Les é - bas, l'a-mour et les jeus,

I' nou' faut aus-si fré-quen - ter Les é - bas, l'a-mour et les jeus,

I' nou' faut aus-si fré-quen - ter Les é - bas, l'a-mour et les jeus,

I' nou' faut ba-ler et chan - ter Jus qu'à tant que nous so - yons mieus

I' nou' faut ba-ler et chan - ter Jus qu'à tant que nous so - yons mieus

I' nou' faut ba-ler et chan - ter Jus qu'à tant que nous so - yons mieus

I' nou' faut ba-ler et chan - ter Jus qu'à tant que nous so - yons mieus

I' nou' faut ba-ler et chan - ter Jus qu'à tant que nous so - yons mieus

Re - voi - cy ve - nir du Prin - temps. L'a - mou - reus le dous et beau temps.

Re - voi - cy ve - nir du Prin - temps. L'a - mou - reus le dous et beau temps.

Re - voi - cy ve - nir du Prin - temps. L'a - mou - reus le dous et beau temps.

Re - voi - cy ve - nir du Prin - temps. L'a - mou - reus le dous et beau temps.

Re - voi - cy ve - nir du Prin - temps. L'a - mou - reus le dous et beau temps.

282   *Claude Lejeune*

Here returns once more the Maytime,
Playful love and lovely playtime.    [Refrain]

All the running streams of springtide,
Seeking summer fields, grow limpid
And the ocean, gently rolling,
Calms the angry storm of winter.
Pretty ducklings plunge and flutter
Play and dive in deep green water
And the cranes, in turning homeward,
Retraverse the skies and vanish.

Refrain

Now the sun, serenely shining
Floods the land in warmth and brightness.
From the clouds the silent shadows
Swiftly pass and change and darken.
All the meadows, woods and hillsides,
With the aid of man, are fertile
And the field uncovers flowers.

Refrain

Love-born Eros, child of beauty,
Yearly sows his flaming nature,
With his magic warmth rekindling all of life
That flies the heavens,
All of life that roams the meadows
All of life that swims the waters.
Even those who never knew him, being lovers,
    melt with pleasure.

Refrain

Let us laugh too and savor
The diverting games of springtide.
All the world, discarding reason
Greets with joy the happy season.

Refrain

# OH CARE, THOU WILT DESPATCH ME

MADRIGAL

THOMAS WEELKES

# YE SACRED MUSES

CONSORT SONG

WILLIAM BYRD

Ye sa - cred Mu - ses, race of Jove,

In mourn-ing weeds,      in mourn-ing weeds

with tears_____ in_____ eyes:_____      Tal - lis is

dead,    Tal - lis is dead,      and Mu - sic dies,

and Mu - - - sic dies.

[40]

In mourn - ing weeds, in

[45]

mourn - ing weeds with tears in eyes:

[50]

Tal - lis is dead, Tal - lis is dead, and Mu -

[55]

- sic dies, and Mu - - - sic

dies, and Mu - sic dies.

292   *William Byrd*

# LACRIMAE ("FLOW MY TEARS")

LUTE SONG

JOHN DOWLAND

ty is fled, And tears, and sighs, and groans my wea - ry
tune is thrown, And fear, and grief, and pain for my de-

days, *my wea - ry days* Of all joys have de - priv - ed.
serts, *for my de-serts* Are my hopes since hope is gone.

Hark you sha - dows that in dark - ness

294 *John Dowland*

dwell, Learn to con-temn light,

Hap - py, hap - py they

that in hell Feel not the world's de - spite.

# TOCCATA

JAN PIETERSZOON SWEELINCK

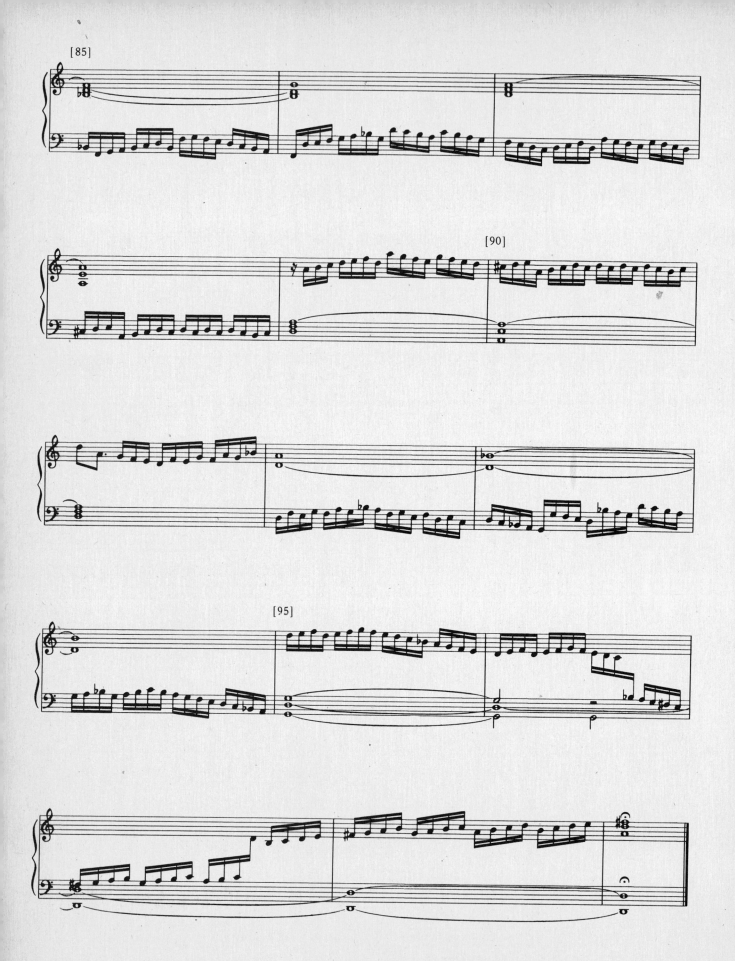

# IN ECCLESIIS

GIOVANNI GABRIELI

(Tenor Solo)

[35]

do - mi - na - ti - o - nis     be - ne - dic,     be - ne -

[40]

dic     a - ni - ma me - a     Do - - - mi -

[45]

num,     Al - le - lu - ia,     Al - le - lu - ia,     Al -

Chorus

Al - le - lu - ia,     Al - le - lu - ia,     Al -

[50]

Sinfonia

Instruments:

Cornetti

Violino (Viola)

Tromboni

(Tenor Solo)

-le - lu - ia.

Al - - - le - lu - ia.

-le - lu - ia.

(Organ)

[55]

(Instruments)

(Organ)

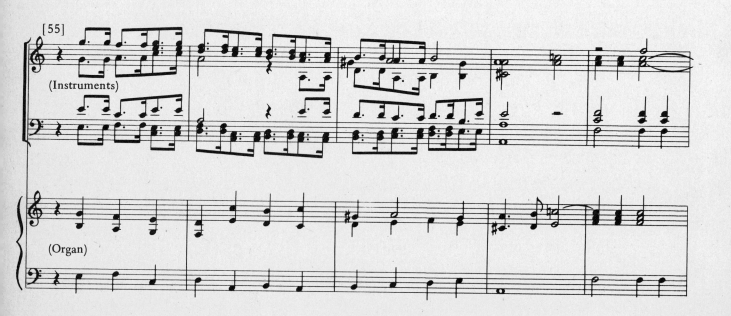

In ecclesiis benedicite Domino. Alleluia!

In omni loco dominationis,
benedic, anima mea, Dominum. Alleluia!

In Deo, salutari meo et gloria mea.
Deus, auxilium meum et spes mea in Deo
 est. Alleluia!

Deus, meus, te invocamus, te adoramus.
Libera nos, salva nos, vivifica nos. Alleluia!

Deus, adjutor noster, in aeternam. Alleluia!

In the churches bless the Lord. Alleluia!

In all places of His dominion,
bless, o my soul, the Lord. Alleluia!

In God is my salvation and my glory.
O God, my help and my hope is in God.
 Alleluia!

O my God, we call upon You, we worship You.
Deliver us, save us, give us life. Alleluia!

O God, our refuge in all eternity. Alleluia!